WORD FINDER

WORD FINDER

PRENTICE-HALL, INC., Englewood Cliffs, N. J.

WORD FINDER

Second Edition

RUTH I. ANDERSON, *Professor*
North Texas State University

LURA LYNN STRAUB, *Professor*
San Diego State College

E. DANA GIBSON, *Professor*
San Diego State College

The spelling, accent, and syllabication of the words most commonly referred to by students, writers, secretaries, printers, and proofreaders

 Library of Congress Catalog Card Number: 64-19987. Printed in the United States of America.

96329-E

ABOUT THIS BOOK

Word Finder, Second Edition, meets the need for a ready-reference book showing (1) all possible places at which words can be divided at ends of lines; (2) the syllabic accent of words; (3) the irregular plurals of nouns; (4) the spelling and capitalization of the words most frequently looked up; and (5) brief definitions of words, such as homonyms, that might be confused with other words. These are the features that caused the first edition of the book to gain immediate popularity. The entire word list, however, has been updated to conform to the most recent trends in word division, pronunciation, and spelling. A thorough analysis of *Webster's Seventh Collegiate Dictionary,* 1963, was made. *Word Finder, Second Edition,* is based on the most modern practices, authoritative sources, and the experiences of the authors. The word list, therefore, includes information most useful to writers, typists, secretaries, clerical workers, and proofreaders.

This book has been designed for quick use, with only two columns of words on each page, alphabetical guides at the head of each page, and a special thumb index. As a further aid to rapid finding, one of the most readable type faces has been used.

The "English Essentials" section, beginning on page 226, gives compact rules for word division, spelling, word usage, number usage, capitalization, and punctuation. The rules are those which the authors have found most effective in teaching English.

The authors are grateful to the many teachers, writers, office managers, secretaries, and others who have made helpful suggestions and comments. As a result of such suggestions, one general change has been made in the present edition. Although division of capitalized words should be avoided, there are times when division is necessary. In this edition, therefore, the dividing points of capitalized words are shown. This edition also includes more past tenses and present participles than the preceding edition. Many words not included in the first edition appear in this revised list.

General supervision of this project was handled by Leonard J. Porter, Educational Book Division, Prentice-Hall, Inc.

The Authors

CONTENTS

WORD
FINDER

A

a·ban′/doned
a·base′
a·bate′
a·bat′ed
ab·bre′/vi/ate
ab·bre′/vi/at′/ing
ab·bre′/vi·a′/tion
ab′di/cate
ab′di/ca′/tion
ab·do′/men
ab·dom′i/nal
ab·duct′
ab·duc′/tion
ab′er/ra′/tion
a·bet′
a·bet′/ted
ab·hor′
ab·horred′
ab·hor′/rence
a·bide′
a·bil′/i·ty (·ties)
ab′ject
ab·jur′/ing
a′ble—/bod′ied
ab·lu′/tion
a′bly
ab′nor/mal′/i·ty
(·ties)
ab·nor′/mal·ly
a·board′
a·bol′/ish
ab′o/li′/tion
a·bom′i/na/ble
a·bom′i/nate
a·bom′i/na′/tion
a·bor′/tive
a·bound′
a·bout′—/face′, *n.*
a·bove′/board′
a·bove′—/men′tioned
ab·ra′/sion
a·breast′
a·bridge′
a·bridg′/ment
a·broad′
ab′ro/gate

ab'ro/ga'/tion
ab·rupt'ly
ab'scess
ab·scond'
ab'sence
ab'sent, *adj.*
ab·sent', *v.*
ab'sen/tee'
ab'sen/tee'/ism
ab·sent/mind'ed
ab'so/lute·ly
ab·solve'
ab·sorb'
ab·sor'/bent
ab·sorp'/tion
ab·stain'
ab·ste'/mi/ous
ab'sti/nence
ab'stract, *n., adj.*
ab·stract', *v.*
ab·stract'ed
ab·surd'
ab·surd'/i·ty (·ties)
a·bun'/dance
a·buse'
a·bu'/sive
a·but'/ment
ac'a/dem'ic
ac·a/de/mi'/cian
a·cad'e·my (/mies)
a cap/pel'la
ac·cede'
ac·cel'/er/ate
ac·cel'/er·a'/tor
ac'cent, *n.*
ac·cent', *v.*
ac·cen'/tu/ate
ac·cept'a/bil'/i·ty
ac·cept'/a·ble
ac·cep'/tance
ac·cept'ed
ac'cess
ac·ces'/si/bil'/i·ty
ac·ces'/si/ble
ac·ces'/so·ry (/ries)
ac'ci/dent
ac'ci/den'/tal·ly
ac·claim'
ac'cla/ma'/tion
ac·cli'/mate
ac·cli'/ma/tize
ac'co/lade'
ac·com'/mo/date
ac·com'/mo/dat'/ing
ac·com'/mo/da'/tion
ac·com'/pa/nies
ac·com'/pa/ni/ment
ac·com'/pa/nist
ac·com'/pa·ny
ac·com'/plice
ac·com'/plish/ment
ac·cor'/dance
ac·cord'/ing·ly
ac·cor'/di·on

ac·cost′
ac·count′
ac·count′a/bil′/i·ty
ac·count′/a·ble
ac·coun′/tan·cy
ac·coun′/tant
ac·cred′it
ac·cred′i/ta′/tion
ac·cru′al
ac·crue′
ac·cru′/ing
ac·cu′/mu/late
ac·cu′/mu/lat/ing
ac·cu′/mu/la′/tion
ac′cu/ra·cy
ac′cu/rate
ac′cu/sa′/tion
ac·cu′/sa/tive
ac·cuse′
ac·cus′/tomed
ac′e/tate
a·ce′/tic
a·cet′y/lene
a·chieve′/ment
ach′/ing·ly
ach′/ro/mat′ic
ac′id
a·cid′i·fy
a·cid′/i·ty (·ties)
ac·knowl′/edge
ac·knowl′/edg/ing
ac·knowl′/edg/ment
a·cous′/ti/cal
a·cous′/tics
ac·quaint′
ac·quaint′/ance/ship
ac′qui/esce′
ac′qui/es′/cence
ac·quire′
ac·quir′/ing
ac′qui/si′/tion
ac·quis′i/tive
ac·quit′
ac·quit′/tal
ac·quit′/ted
a′cre/age
ac′rid
ac′ri/mo′/ni/ous
ac′ro/bat′ic
a·cross′
act′/ing
ac′tion/a·ble
ac′ti/vate
ac′tive·ly
ac·tiv′/i·ty (·ties)
ac′tor
ac′tu/al′/i·ty (·ties)
ac′tu/al·ly
ac′tu/ar′i·al
ac′tu/ar′y (/ies)
a·cu′/i·ty
a·cu′/men
a·cute′/ness
ad′age

a·da'/gio (/gios)
ad'a/mant
a·dapt' (make suitable)
a·dapt'/a·ble
a·dapt'a/bil'/i·ty
ad'ap/ta'/tion
ad·dict', *v.*
ad'dict, *n.*
ad·dic'/tion
ad·di'/tion·al
ad'di/tive
ad·dress'
ad'dress·ee'
Ad·dres'/so/graph
ad·duce'
ad'e/noid
ad'ept, *n.* (an expert)
a·dept', *adj.* (proficient)
ad'e/qua·cy
ad'e/quate·ly
ad·here'
ad·her'/ence
ad·her'/ing
ad·he'/sion
ad·he'/sive/ness
a·dieu'
ad in'fi/ni'/tum
ad in'ter·im
ad·ja'/cent
ad'jec/ti'val
ad'jec/tive
ad·join'
ad·journ'/ment
ad·judge'
ad·ju'/di/cate
ad·ju'/di/ca'/tion
ad'junct
ad'ju/ra'/tion
ad·jure'
ad·just'/a·ble
ad·just'er
ad·just'/ment
ad'ju/tant
ad'—/lib'
ad·min'/is/ter
ad·min'/is/trate
ad·min'/is/tra'/tion
ad·min'/is/tra'/tor
ad'mi/ra/ble
ad'mi/ral·ty (/ties)
ad'mi/ra'/tion
ad·mire'
ad·mir'/ing·ly
ad·mis'/si/ble
ad·mis'/sion
ad·mit'/tance
ad·mit'/ting
ad·mon'/ish
ad'mo/ni'/tion
a·do'be
ad'o/les'/cence
a·dopt' (choose)
a·dop'/tion

a·dor'/a·ble
ad'o/ra'/tion
a·dorn'/ment
a·dre'/nal
a·dren'a/line
a·droit'
ad'u/la'/tion
a·dult'
a·dul'/ter·y (/ies)
a·dult'/hood
ad va·lo'/rem
ad·vanced'
ad·vance'/ment
ad·vanc'/ing
ad·van'/tage
ad'van/ta'/geous·ly
ad'ven/ti'/tious
ad·ven'/ture
ad·ven'/tur/ous
ad'verb
ad·ver'/bi·al
ad'ver/sar'y (/ies)
ad·verse'ly
ad·ver'/si·ty (/ties)
ad·ver'/tise/ment
ad'ver/tis'er
ad·vice', *n.*
ad·vis'a/bil'/i·ty
ad·vis'/a·ble
ad·vise', *v.*
ad·vised'
ad·vis'/ed·ly
ad·vise'/ment
ad·vis'er
ad·vi'/so·ry
ad'vo/ca·cy
ad'vo/cate
a·e'ri·al
aer·o/dy/nam'/ics
aer'o/naut
aes/thet'/ics
af'fa/bil'/i·ty
af'fa/ble
af·fair'
af·fect', *v*
(to influence)
af'fec/ta'/tion
af·fect'/ed/ness
af·fec'/tion/ate·ly
af·fi'/ance
af'fi/da'/vit
af·fil'i/ate
af·fil'i/a'tion
af·fin'/i·ty (·ties)
af·firm'
af'fir/ma'/tion
af·fir'/ma/tive
af·fix'
af·flict'
af·flic'/tion
af'flu/ence
af·ford'
af·front'
a·fore'/said'

aft′er
aft′er—/din′ner, *adj.*
aft′er/math
aft′er/noon′
aft′er/thought′
aft′er/ward
a·gainst′
a′gen·cy (/cies)
a·gen′da, *pl.*
(*sing.*/dum)
a′gent
ag′gra/vate
ag′gra/vat′/ing·ly
ag′gra/va′/tion
ag′gre/gate
ag′gre/gat/ing
ag·gres′/sion
ag·gres′/sive/ness
ag·gres′/sor
ag·grieved′
a·ghast′
ag′ile·ly
a·gil′/i·ty
ag′i/tate
ag′i/ta′/tion
ag′i/ta′/tor
ag·nos′/tic
ag·nos′/ti/cism
ag′o/niz/ing
ag′o·ny (/nies)
a·grar′i·an
a·gree′a/bil′/i·ty
a·gree′/a·ble/ness
a·greed′
a·gree′/ment
ag′ri/cul′/tur·al
ag′ri/cul′/ture
a·gron′o/mist
a·gron′o·my
a·ground′
a·head′
aim′/less/ness
air base
air′—/con·di′tioned
air′ con/di′/tion/ing
air′—/cooled′
air′/craft′, *sing. & pl.*
air′/field′
air′ force′
air′/lift′
air′/line′
air′/mail′
air′/plane′
air′ pock·et
air′/port′
air′/ship′
air′/sick/ness
air′/strip′
air′/tight′
air′/wor′/thy
air′/wor′/thi/ness
aisle
al′a/bas′/ter
à la carte

a·lac'/ri·ty
à la mode'
a·larm'/ing·ly
a·larm'/ist
al·bi'no (/nos)
al'bum
al·bu'/men
Al'bu/quer'/que
al'co/hol'ic
al'co/hol/ism
al'cove
al'der/man (/men)
al·fal'fa
al'ge/bra
al'ge/bra'ic
a'li·as
al'i·bi
al'ien
al'ien/ate
a·lign'/ment
a·like'
al'i/men'/ta·ry
al'i/mo'ny
al'i/quot
al'ka·li
al'ka/line
al'ka/lin'/i·ty
al·lay'/ing
al·lege'
al·leg'/ed·ly
Al'le/ghe'ny (/nies)
al·le'/giance
al'le/go'ry (/ries)
al·le'/gro (/gros)
al·ler'/gic
al'ler·gy (/gies)
al·le'/vi/ate
al'ley (·leys)
al·li'/ance
al·lied'
al'lo/cate
al'lo/ca'/tion
al·lot'/ment
al·lot'/ted
all out, *adv.*
all'/out', *adj.*
all'/o'ver, *adj.*
al·low'/ance
al·loy', *v.*
all right
al·lude' (refer to)
al·lu'/sion
al·ly' (·lies'), *v.*
al·ly'/ing
Al'ma Ma'ter
al'ma/nac
al·might'y
al'mond
al'most
a·long'/side'
a·loud'
al'pha/bet
al'pha/bet'/i·cal·ly
al'pha/bet/ize

al·read′y (at this time)
al′tar
al′ter, *v.* (to change)
al′ter·a′/tion
al′ter/ca′/tion
al′ter/nate
al·ter′/na/tive
al·though′
al′ti/tude
al′to/geth′er (entirely)
al′tru/ism
a·lu′/mi/num
a·lum′na (/nae), *fem.*
a·lum′/nus (·ni), *masc.*
al′ways
a·mal′/ga/mate
a·mal′/ga/ma′/tion
a·man′u/en′/sis (/ses)
am′a/teur′/ish
a·maze′/ment
Am′a/zon
am·bas′/sa/dor
am′bi/dex′/trous
am′bi/gu′/i·ty (·ties)
am·big′u/ous·ly
am·bi′/tion
am·bi′/tious
am′bu/lance
am′bu/la/to′ry
am′bush
a·me′/lio/rate
a·me′/na/ble
a·mend′/ment
a·me′/ni·ty (·ties)
A·mer′i/can
am′e/thyst
a′mi·a/bil′/i·ty
a′mi/a·ble
am′i/ca/bil′/i·ty
am′i/ca/ble
am′i·ty (·ties)
am·mo′/ni·a
am′mu/ni′/tion
am·ne′/si·a
am′nes·ty (/ties)
a·moe′ba (/bae; /bas)
a·mong′
a·mor′al
am′o/rous
a·mor′/phous
am′or/ti/za′/tion
am′or/tize
a·mount′
am′per/age
am′pere
am′per/sand
am·phib′i·an
am·phib′i/ous
am′phi/the′a/ter
am′ple
am′pli/fi/ca′/tion
am′pli/fi′er
am′pli·fy

am'pli/tude
am'ply
am'pu/tate
am'pu/ta'/tion
am'pu/tee'
a·muse'/ment
a·mus'/ing·ly
an'a/log'/i·cal
a·nal'o/gous
an'a/logue
a·nal'o·gy (/gies)
a·nal'y/sis (/ses)
an'a/lyst
an'a/lyt'/i·cal
an'a/lyze
an'a/lyz/ing
an'ar/chism
an'ar/chy
a·nath'e·ma
an'a/tom'/i·cal
a·nat'o·my (/mies)
an'ces'/tor
an·ces'/tral
an'ces'/try (/tries)
an'chor/age
an·cho'vy (/vies)
an'cient
an'cil/lar'y
an·dan'te
and'/i'ron
an'ec/do'/tal
an'ec/dote
a·ne'/mi·a
a·ne'/mic
an'es/the'/si·a
an'es/thet'ic
an·es'/the/tist
an·es'/the/tize
an·gel'ic
an'ger
an·gi'na pec'/to/ris
an'gel
An·go'ra
an'gri·ly
an'gri/ness
an'gry
an'guish
an'gu/lar
an'i/line
an'i/mal/ism
an'i/mate
an'i/mat'/ed·ly
an'i/ma'/tion
an'i/mos'/i·ty (·ties)
an'kle
an'kle/bone'
an'nal/ist
an·nex', *v.*
an'nex·a'/tion
an·ni'/hi/late
an·ni'/hi/la'/tion
an'ni/ver'/sa·ry (/ries)
an'no/tate
an'no/ta'/tion

an · nounce′
an · nounc′er
an · noy′/ance
an · noyed′
an′nu · al
an · nu′i/tant
an · nu′/i · ty (· ties)
an · nul′
an · nulled′
an · nul′/ling
a · noint′
a · nom′a/lous
a · nom′a · ly (/lies)
a · non′y/mous
an · oth′er
an′swer/a · ble
an · tag′o/nism
an · tag′o/nist
an · tag′o/nis′/tic
an · tag′o/nize
ant/arc′/tic
an′te/ced′/ent
an′te/date′
an · te me · ri′/di · em
an · ten′na (/nae; /nas)
an · te′/ri · or
an′them
an · thol′o · gy (/gies)
an′thra/cite
an′thrax
an′thro/pol′o · gy
an′ti/air′/craft′
an′ti/bi/ot′ic
an · tic′i/pate
an · tic′i/pa′/tion
an′ti/cli/mac′/tic
an′ti/cli′/max
an′ti/dote
an′ti/freeze′
an′ti/his′/ta/mine
an · tip′a/thy (/thies)
an′ti/quar′i · an
an′ti/quar′y (/ies)
an′ti/quat′ed
an · tique′
an · tiq′/ui · ty (/ties)
an′ti/sep′tic
an′ · ti/so′/cial
an · tith′e/sis (/ses)
an′ti/tox′in
an′to/nym
anx · i′/e · ty (· ties)
anx′/ious
an′y/bod′y
an′y/how
an′y/one
an′y/thing
an′y/way
an′y/where
a · or′ta (/tas; /tae)
a · part′/ment
ap′a/thet′ic
ap′a/thy (/thies)
ap′er/ture

a'pex
a·pha'/si·a
a'phid
aph'o·rism
a'pi/ar'y (/ies)
a·piece'
a·pol'o/get'ic
a·pol'o/get'/i·cal·ly
a·pol'o/gize
a·pol'o·gy (/gies)
ap'o/plec'/tic
ap'o/plex'y
a·pos'/tle
ap'os/tol'ic
a·pos'/tro/phe
a·poth'e/car'y (/ies)
Ap·pa/la'/chian
ap·pall'/ing
ap'pa/ra'/tus
(/tus; /tus·es)
ap·par'el
ap·par'/ent
ap'pa/ri'/tion
ap·peal'
ap·pear'/ance
ap·pease'
ap·pel'/late
ap'pel/la'tion
ap'pel/lee'
ap·pen'/dage
ap'pen/dec'/to·my
(/mies)
ap·pen'/di/ci'tis
ap·pen'/dix
(/dix·es; /di/ces)
ap'per/ceive'
ap'per/cep'/tion
ap'per/tain'
ap'pe/tite
ap'pe/tiz'/ing
ap·plaud'
ap·plause'
ap·pli'/ance
ap'pli/ca/bil'/i·ty
ap'pli/ca/ble
ap'pli/cant
ap'pli/ca'/tion
ap·plied'
ap'pli/qué'
ap·ply'/ing
ap·point'/ment
ap·por'/tion/ment
ap'po/si'/tion
ap·pos'i/tive
ap/prais'al
ap·praise'
ap·prais'/ing
ap·pre'/cia/ble
ap·pre'/ci/ate
ap·pre'/ci·a'/tion
ap'pre/hend'
ap'pre/hen'/si/ble
ap'pre/hen'/sive
ap·pren'/tice

ap·pren′/tice/ship
ap·prise′
ap·proach′
ap′pro/ba′/tion
ap·pro′/pri/ate·ly
ap·pro′/pri/ate/ness
ap·pro′/pri·a′/tion
ap·prov′al
ap·prox′i/mate
ap·prox′i/ma′/tion
ap·pur′/te/nance
ap′ri/cot
a pri·o′ri
ap′ro/pos′
ap′ti/tude
apt′/ness
aq′ua
aq′ua/cade
aq′ua/ma/rine′
a·quar′i·um
(/ums; ·i·a)
a·quat′ic
aq′ue/duct
Ar′a/bic
ar′a·ble
ar′bi/ter
ar′bi/tra/ble
ar′bi/trar′i·ly
ar′bi/trar′y
ar′bi/trate
ar′bi/tra′/tion
ar′bi/tra′/tor
ar·bo′/re/ous
ar·bo/re′/tum
(/tums; ·ta)
ar·cade′
ar′chae·o/log′/i·cal
ar′chae/ol′o/gist
ar′chae/ol′o·gy
ar·cha′ic
arch′/er·y
ar′chi/tect
ar′chi/tec′/tur·al
ar′chi/tec′/ture
ar′chives, *pl.*
arch′/way′
arc′/tic
ar′dent
ar′dor
ar′du/ous
ar′e·a (region)
a·re′na
Ar′gen/ti′na
ar′gued
ar′gu/ment
ar′gu/men′/ta/tive
a′ri·a (solo melody)
ar′id
a·rid′/i·ty
ar′is/toc′/ra·cy (/cies)
a·ris′/to/crat
a·rith′/me/tic
ar′ith/met′/i·cal
ar′ma/ment

ar′ma/ture
arm′/chair′
arm′/ful (/fuls)
ar′mi/stice
ar′mor·y (/ies)
ar′my (·mies)
a·ro′ma
ar′o/mat′ic
a·round′
a·rouse′
ar·peg′/gio (/gios)
ar·raign′/ment
ar·range′/ment
ar·rang′/ing
ar·rayed′
ar·ray′/ing
ar·rears′, *pl.*
ar·rest′
ar·riv′al
ar·rive′
ar′ro/gance
ar′se/nal
ar′se/nic
ar′son
ar·te′/ri·al
ar·te′/ri·o/scle/ro′/sis
ar′ter·y (/ies)
ar·te′/sian well
art′/ful·ly
ar·thri′/tis
ar′ti/cle
ar·tic′u/late
ar·tic′u/la′tion
ar′ti/fice
ar′ti/fi′/cial
ar′ti/fi′/ci/al′/i·ty (·ties)
ar·til′/ler·y
ar′ti/san (mechanic)
art′/ist
ar·tis′/tic
as·bes′/tos
as·cend′
as·cen′/dan·cy
as·cen′/dant
as·cen′/sion
as·cent′ (a rising)
as′cer/tain′
as′cer/tain′/a·ble
as·cet′ic
as·cet′i/cism
a·shamed′
A′sian
A′si/at′ic
a·side′
as′i/nine
a·sleep′
as·par′a/gus
as′pect
as·per′/i·ty (·ties)
as·per′/sion
as′phalt
as·phyx′i/ate
as·phyx′i/at/ing

as·phyx′i/a′tion
as′pic
as′pi/rant
as′pi/ra′/tion
as·pire′
as′pi/rin
as·sail′
as·sail′/ant
as·sas′/sin
as·sas′/si/nate
as·sas′/si/na′/tion
as·sault′
as·sayed′
as·say′/ing
as·sem′/ble
as·sem′/bly (/blies)
as·sent′ (consent)
as·sert′
as·ser′/tion
as·ser′/tive/ness
as·sess′/a·ble
as·sess′/ment
as·ses′/sor
as′set
as·sid′u/ous/ness
as·sign′
as·sign′/a·ble
as′sig/na′/tion
as′sign·ee′
as·sign′er
as·sign′/ment
as·sim′i/late
as·sim′i/la′/tion
as·sist′
as·sis′/tance
as·size′
as·so′/ci/ate
as·so′/ci·a′/tion
as·sort′/ment
as·suage′
as·suag′/ing
as·sume′
as·sump′/sit
as·sump′/tion
as·sur′/ance
as·sure′
as·sur′/ed·ly
as′ter/isk
asth′ma
a·stig′/ma/tism
as·ton′/ish/ment
as·tound′
as·trin′/gent
as·trol′o/ger
as·trol′o·gy
as′tro/naut
as·tron′o/mer
as′tro/nom′/i·cal
as·tron′o·my
as·tute′
a·sy′/lum
a·sym′/me/try
a′the/ism
a′the/ist

a'the/is'/tic
ath'/lete
ath/let'/ics
At·lan'/tic
at'las
at'mo/sphere
at'mos/pher'ic
at'om
a·tom'ic
a·tro'/cious
a·troc'/i·ty (·ties)
at'ro/phied
at'ro/phy
at'ta/ché'
at·tach'/ment
at·tack'
at·tain'/a·ble
at·tain'/ment
at·tempt'
at·ten'/dance
at·ten'/dant
at·ten'/tion
at·ten'/tive
at·ten'u/a'tion
at·test'
at'tes/ta'/tion
at·tire'
at'ti/tude
at·tor'/ney (/neys)
at·tor'/neys at law
at·tract'
at·trac'/tion
at·trac'/tive
at·trib'/ute, *v.*
at'tri/bute, *n.*
at·tri'/tion
at·tune'
a·typ'/i·cal
au'burn
auc'/tion
auc'/tion/eer'
au·da'/cious
au·dac'/i·ty
au'di/bil'/i·ty
au'di/ble
au'di/ence
au'di/om'e/ter
au'di·o/vis'u·al
au'dit
au·di'/tion
au'di/tor
au'di/to'ri·um
(/ums; /ri·a)
au'di/to'ry
aug/ment', *v.*
aug'/ment, *n.*
au·gust'
au'ra
au're·o/my'/cin
au re·voir'
au'ric
au'ri/cle
au·ric'u/lar
au·ro'ra

aus/pi'/cious
aus/tere'
aus/ter'/i·ty (·ties)
Aus/tral'/ian
Aus'/tri·an
au·then'/tic
au'then/tic'/i·ty
au'thor
au·thor'i/ta'/tive/ness
au·thor'/i·ty (·ties)
au'tho/ri/za'/tion
au'tho/rize
au'thor/ship
au'to/bi/og'/ra/phy
(/phies)
au'to/bi'o/graph'/i·cal
au·toc'/ra·cy (/cies)
au'to/crat
au'to/crat'ic
au'to/graph
au'to/mat'ic
au'to/mat·ed
au'to/mat'/i·cal·ly
au'to/ma'/tion
au·tom'a/ton
au·to/mo/bile'
au'to/mo'/tive
au·ton'o/mous
au·ton'o·my (/mies)
au'top·sy (/sies)
au'to/sug/ges'/tion
au'tumn
aux/il'/ia·ry (/ries)
a·vail'a/bil'/·ty
(·ties)
a·vail'/a·ble
av'a/lanche
av'a/rice
av'a/ri'/cious
a·venge'
av'e/nue
av'er/age
a·verred'
a·ver'/ring
a·verse'
a·ver'/sion
a·vert'
a'vi/ar'y (/ies)
a'vi·a'/tion
a'vi·a'/tor
av'id
av'o/ca'do (/dos)
av'o/ca'/tion
a·void'/a·ble
a·void'/ance
av'oir/du/pois'
a·wait'
a·wake'
a·wak'/en/ing
a·ward'
a·ware'/ness
a·way'
aw'ful
a·while'

awk'/ward
aw'ning
a·woke'
ax'i·om
ax'i/o·mat'ic
ax'is (ax'es)
ax'le
Ax'min'/ster
a·za'/lea
az'ure

B

ba'by (·bies)
bac'/ca/lau'/re/ate
bach'e/lor
ba·cil'/lus (·li)
back'/bone'
back'/door'
back'/fire'
back'/ground'
back'/hand'ed
back'/log'
back'/slide
back'/stage'
back'/stop'
back'/ward/ness
ba'con
bac/te'/ri·um (/ri·a)
bac/te'/ri·al
bac/te'/ri/ol'o·gy
bad'/ger
bad'i/nage'
bad'/min'/ton
baf'/fle
baf'/fling
bag'/gage
bailed
bail'ee'
bai'/liff
bai'/li/wick
bail'/ment
bail'or'
Ba'ke·lite
bak'/er·y (/ies)
bak'/ing
bal'/ance
bal'/co·ny (/nies)
bald'—/head'ed
baled
bal'/ing
balk
bal'/lad
bal'/last
bal'/le/ri'na
bal'/let
bal/lis'/tics

bal/loon′
bal′/lot
ball′—/point′
ball′/room′
balm′i/ness
Bal′/tic
bal′/us/trade′
bam/bi′no (/nos; ·ni)
bam/boo′
ba·nal′/i·ty
ba·nan′·a
ban′/dage
ban′/dag/ing
ban/dan′na
band′/box′
ban/deau′ (/deaux′)
ban′/dit
ban′/ish/ment
ban′/is/ter
ban′/jo (/jos)
bank′/book
bank′er
bank note
bank′/rupt·cy (/cies)
ban′/ner
ban′/quet
ban′/tam
ban′/ter
bap′/tism
Bap′/tist
bap/tize′
bar/bar′i·an
bar/bar′ic
bar′/be/cue
barbed
bar′/ber
bar/bi′/tu/rate
barb′/wire′
bare′/back′
bare′/faced′
bare′/foot′
bare′/head′ed
bare′ly
bar′/gain
bar′i/tone
bar′/keep′er
bar′ley
barn′/storm′
barn′/yard′
ba·rom′e/ter
bar′o/met′/ric
ba·roque′
bar′/rack
bar/rage′
bar′/rel
bar′/ren
bar′/ri/cade′
bar′/ri·er
bar′/ris/ter
bar′/room′
bar′/ter
base′/ball′
base′/board′
base′/less

base'/ment
bash'/ful/ness
ba'·sic
ba'si/cal·ly
ba'sin
bas'/si/net'
ba'sis (·ses)
bas'/ket/ball'
bas'—/re·lief'
bas/soon'
bass'/wood'
bath, *n.*
bathe, *v.*
bath'/ing
bath'/robe
bath'/room
ba·tiste'
ba·ton'
Bat'on Rouge, La.
bat/tal'/ion
bat'/ter
bat'/ter·y (/ies)
bat'tle/field'
bat'tle/ground'
bat'/tle/ship'
baux'/ite
Ba·var'·i·an
bay'o/net
Ba'yonne', N. J.
bay'ou
ba·zaar' (market place)
beach'/head'

bea'/con
bear'/a·ble
beau (beaux)
beau'/te/ous
beau/ti'/cian
beau'/ti/fied
beau'/ti/ful
beau'/ti/fy'/ing
beau'ty (/ties)
bea'/ver
be·came'
be·cause'
beck'on
be·come'
bed'/ding
bed'/lam
be·drag'/gle
bed'/rock'
bed'/roll'
bed'/room'
bed'/side'
bed'/spread'
beech'/nut'
beef'/steak'
be·fore'
be·fore'/hand'
be·friend'
be·gin'
be·gin'/ning
be·go'/ni·a
be·grudge'
be·guile'

be·gun'
be·half'
be·have'
be·hav'/ing
be·hav'/ior
be·held'
be·hind'
be·hind'/hand'
be·hold'
be·hoove'
beige
be·lat'ed
bel'/fry (/fries)
Bel'/gian
be·lief'
be·liev'/a·ble
be·lieve'
be·liev'/ing
be·lit'/tle
bell'/boy'
bell'/hop'
bel'/li/cose
bel/lig'/er/ence
be·long'
be·lov'ed
be·low'
belt'ed
be·neath'
ben'e/dic'/tion
ben'e/fac'/tor
be·nef'i/cence
be·nef'i/cent·ly
ben'e/fi'/cial
ben'e/fi'/ci/ar'y (/ies)
ben'e/fit
ben'e/fit'ed
ben'e/fit'/ing
be·nev'o/lence
be·nev'o/lent·ly
ben'/ga/line
be·nign'
be·nig'/nant
ben'/zene
be·queath'
be·quest'
be·reave'/ment
be·ret'
Berke'/ley, Calif.
Berk'/ley, Mich.
ber'ry (/ries)
ber'/serk
berth (assigned space)
be·seech'
be·side'
be·sides'
be·siege'
be·stow'
be·tray'al
be·troth'al
bet'/ter
bet'/ter/ment
be·tween'
be·tween'/times'
bev'el

bev′/eled
bev′/er/age
bev′y (/ies)
be·ware′
be·wil′/dered
be·wil′/der/ment
be·yond′
bi·an′/nu·al
(twice a year)
bi′ased
bi·ax′i·al
Bi′ble
Bib′/li·cal
bib′/li/og′/ra/pher
bib′/li·o/graph′/i·cal
bib′/li/og′ra/phy
(/phies)
bib′u/lous
bi·cam′/er·al
bi·car′/bon/ate
bi·cen/te′/na·ry (/ries)
bi′cen/ten′/ni·al
bi′ceps, *sing. & pl.*
bick′er
bi·cus′/pid
bi′cy/cle
bi′cy/clist
bid′/da/ble
bi·en′/ni·al
(every two years)
bi·en′/ni·um (/ni·a)
(two years)

bi·fo′/cal
big′a/mist
big′a·my (/mies)
big′/ot·ed
big′/ot·ry (/ries)
big′/wig′
bi·la′/bi·al
bi·lat′/er·al
bi·lin′/gual
bi·lin′/guist
bil′/ious
bill′/board′
bil′/let
bill′/fold′
bil′/liards
bil′/lion
bil′/lion/aire′
bi′me/tal′/lic
bi·met′/al/lism
bi·month′ly (/lies)
bi′na·ry
bind′er
bind′/er·y (/ies)
bin/oc′u/lar
bi·no′/mi·al
bi·og′/ra/pher
bi′o/graph′ic
bi′o/graph′/i·cal
bi·og′/ra/phy (/phies)
bi′o/log′/i·cal
bi·ol′o/gist
bi·ol′o·gy

bi·par'/ti/san
bi'ped
bi'plane'
bird'/house'
bird'ie
bird's'—/eye', *n., adj.*
birth'/day'
birth'/mark'
birth'/place'
birth'/right'
birth'/stone'
bis'/cuit
bi'sect'
bi·sec'/tion·al
bish'op
Bis'/marck, N. D.
bi'son, *sing. & pl.*
bit'/ing·ly
bit'/ter/ness
bit'/ter/sweet'
bi·tu'/men
bi·tu'/mi/nous
biv'/ouac
biv'/ouacked
bi·week'ly (/lies)
bi·zarre' (fantastic)
black'/ber'ry (/ries)
black'/bird'
black'/board'
black'/ened
black'/jack
black'/list
black'/mail'
black'—/mar'ket, *v.*
black'/ness
black'/out'
blad'/der
blamed
blame'/less
blanch
blan'/dish/ment
blan'/ket
blank'/ness
bla·sé'
blas/pheme'
blas'/phe/mous
blas'/phe·my (/mies)
blast'ed
blast'/off, *n., adj.*
bla'/tan·cy
bla'/tant
bleach'/ers, *pl.*
bleak'ly
bleed'er
blem'/ish
blend'ed
bless'/ed/ness
blight
blimp
blind'/fold'
blind'/ness
blink'er
bliss'/ful
blis'/ter

ılithe
ılitz'/krieg'
ıliz'/zard
ıloc
ılock/ade'
ılock'head'
ılond'/ness
ılood'ed
ılood'/hound'
ılood'i/est
ılood'i/ness
ılood poi'/son/ing
ılood pres'/sure
blood'/shed'
blood'/shot'
blood'/stained'
blood'/thirst'y
blood ves'/sel
blood'y
bloom'/ing
blos'/som
blotch'y
blot'/ter
blouses
blow'er
blow'/out'
blow'/torch'
blue'/ber'ry (/ries)
blue'/bird'
blue blood
blue'/bon'/net
blue'/grass'
blue jay
blue'—/pen'cil, *v.*
blue'/print'
bluff'er
blu'/ing
blu'/ish
blun'/der
blunt'ly
blurb
blus'/ter
blus'/ter · y
board'er
board'/ing/house'
board'/ing school
board'/walk'
boast'/ful
boast'/ing · ly
boat'/swain
bob'/bin
bob'by—/sox'er
bob'/cat'
bob'/sled'
bod'/ice
bod'i · ly
bod'y (/ies)
bod'y/guard'
Bo · he'/mi · an
boil'er
Boi'se, Idaho
bois'/ter/ous
bold'/face', *n.*
bold'—/faced', *adj.*

bold′ly
bold′/ness
bo·le′ro (/ros)
Bo·liv′i·an
boll weev′·il
Bo·lo′/gna
bo·lo′/ney
Bol′she/vism
bol′/ster
bomb
bom/bard′
bom′/bard/ier′
bom/bard′/ment
bom/bas′/tic
bomb′er
bomb′/shell′
bomb′/sight′
bo′na fide
bo·nan′za
bon′/bon′
bond′/age
bond′/hold′er
bond′/ing
bon′/fire′
bon′go
bon′/net
bon′ny
bo′nus
bon voy′/age′
boo′by (/bies)
boo′by trap
boo′gie—/woo′gie
book′/bind′/er·y (/ies)
book′/case′
book′/end
book′ie
book′/keep′er
book′/keep′/ing
book′/let
book′/mark′
book′/mo/bile
book′/shelf′ (/shelves′)
book′/shop′
book′/store′
book′/worm′
boo′/mer/ang
boor′/ish/ness
boost′ed
boo′/tee′ (infant's boot)
boot′/leg′
boo′ty (plunder)
booze
bo·rac′ic
bo′rax
bor′/der
bor′/der/line′, *adj.*
bo′re·al
bore′/dom
bo′ric
bor′/ing
bor′/ough
bor′/row

o′·som
o·tan′/i·cal
ot′a/nist
ot′a·ny
otch′y
oth′er
oth′/er/some
ot′/tled
ot′/tle/neck′
ot′/tler
ot′/tling
ot′/tom
ot′/tom/less
ou′/doir
ouf′/fant
ough
ought
ouil′/lon (broth)
oul′/der
ou′/le/vard
ounc′/ing
ound′a·ry (/ries)
ound′/less
oun′/te/ous
oun′/ti/ful
oun′ty (/ties)
ou/quet′
our′/bon
our′/geois, *sing. & pl.*
our/geoi′/sie′
ou′/ton/niere′
o′vine

bow′el
bow′/knot′
bow′/leg′/ged
bowl′er
bowl′/ing
box′/car′
box′er
box′/ing
box′/wood′
boy′/cott
boy′/hood
boy′/ish/ness
brace′/let
brac′er
brack′et
brag′/gart
brag′/ging
Braille
brain′i/ness
brain′/less
brain′/sick′/ness
brain′/storm′
brain′/wash′/ing
brake′/man (/men)
bram′/ble
bran′/died
bran′/dish
brand′—/new′
bran′dy (/dies)
brass′y
bra/va′do (/does)
brav′/er·y

bra'vo (/vos)
brawn'i/ness
brawn'y
bra'/zen
Bra/zil'/ian
breach
bread'—/and—
/but'ter, *adj.*
bread'/stuff'
breadth
bread'/win'/ner
break'/a · ble
break'/age
break'/down'
break'/fast
break'/through'
break'/wa'/ter
breast'/bone'
breath, *n.*
breathe, *v.*
breath'er
breath'/ing
breath'/less/ness
breath'/tak'/ing
breath'y
breech
breed'/ing
breeze
breez'i/ness
breez'y
breth'/ren
(a *pl.* of brother)
breve
bre'/vi/ar'y (/ies)
brev'/i · ty (· ties)
brew'/er · y (/ies)
brib'/er · y (/ies)
brib'/ing
bric'—a—/brac'
brick'/kiln'
brick'/lay'er
brick'/work'
brid'al, *adj.*
bride'/groom
brides'/maid'
bridge'/work'
bri'/dle, *n.*
brief'/case'
bri'er
bri/gade'
brig'a/dier'
bright'en
bril'/liance
bril'/lian · cy
bril'/lian/tine'
bril'/liant · ly
brim'/ful'
brim'/ming
bri/quette'
bris'/tle
bris'/tling
Brit'/ain (place)
Brit'i/cism
Brit'/ish · er

Brit'on (person)
brit'/tle
broach
broad'/cast'
broad'/cloth'
broad'en
broad'ly
broad—/mind'ed · ness
broad'/side'
bro/cade'
broc'/co · li
bro/chure'
brogue
broil'er
bro'ken/heart'ed
bro'/ker
bro'/ker/age
bro'/mide
bro'/mine
bron'/chi · al
bron/chi'/tis
bronze
brooch
brood'er
brook'/let
Brook'/line, Mass.
Brook'/lyn, N. Y.
broth'er
broth'/er/hood
broth'er—/in—/law'
(broth'ers— . . .)
broth'/er · ly
brow'/beat'
brown'/ish
browse
bru'in
bruise
bruis'/ing
bru/net', *masc.*
bru/nette', *fem.*
brunt
brush'—/off', *n.*
brusque
bru'/tal
bru/tal'/i · ty (· ties)
brut'/ish
Bryn' Mawr', Pa.
bub'/ble
buck'a/roo' (/roos')
buck'/et/ful (/fuls)
buck'et seat
buck'eye'
buck'le
buck'/ling
buck'/ram
buck'/shot'
buck'/skin'
buck'/wheat'
bu · col'ic
Bud'/dha
Bud'/dhism
bud'dy (/dies)
budg'/et · ed
budg'/et/ing

Bue′/nos Air′es
buf′/fa · lo (/loes; · lo)
buff′er
buf/fet′
buf/foon′
bug′a/boo′ (/boos′)
bug′/bear′
bu′gle
build′er
build′/ing
bul′/bar
bul′/bous
Bul/gar′i · an
bulge
bulg′/ing
bulk′/head′
bulk′i/ness
bulk′y
bull′/dog′
bull′/doz′er
bul′/let
bul′/le/tin
bul′/let/proof′
bull′/fight′er
bull′/frog′
bull′/head′ed
bul′/lion
(gold and silver)
bul′/lock
bull's′—/eye′, *n.*
bul′ly (/lies)
bul′/wark
bum′/ble/bee′
bump′er
bump′i/ness
bump′y
bun′/dle
bun′/ga/low
bun′/gled
bun′/gling
bun′/ion
bunk′/house′
bun′ny, (/nies)
bun′/ting
buoy
buoy′/an · cy
buoy′/ant
bur′/den/some
bu′reau
bu · reauc′/ra · cy
(/cies)
bu′reau/crat
bur′/glar
bur′/glar/ize
bur′/gla · ry (/ries)
bur′i · al
bur′/ied
bur′/lap
bur/lesque′
bur′ly
bur′/li/ness
burn′er
bur′/nish · er
bur′ro (/ros)

bur'/row
bur'/sar
bur/si'/tis
bur'y/ing
bus (bus·es)
bush'el
bush'/ing
bus'/ied
bus'i/est
bus'i·ly
busi'/ness
busi'/ness/like'
busi'/ness/man'
(/men')
bus'/tle
bus'/tling
bus'y
bus'y/bod'y (/ies)
bu'tane
butch'er
butt
Butte, Mont.
but'/ter
but'/ter/fat'
but'/ter/fin'/gers
but'/ter/fly'
but'/ter/milk'
but'/ter/nut'
but'/ter/scotch'
but'/ton
but'/ton/hole'
but'/tress
bux'om
buy'er
buz'/zard
buzz bomb
buzz'er
buzz saw
by'-and-by', *n.*
by'gone'
by'law'
by'—/line'
by'pass'
by'play'
by'—/prod'uct
by'stand'er
by'word'

C

ca'bal/le'ro (/ros)
ca·ba'na
cab'a/ret
cab'/bage
cab'in
cab'i/net

ca'ble/gram
ca·boose'
ca·ca'o (·os)
cache
cack'le
cac'/tus (·ti; /tus·es)
ca·dav'er
cad'/die
ca'dence
ca·den'za
ca·det'
ca·du'/ce·us (/ce·i)
ca·fé'
caf'e/te'/ri·a
caf'/feine
cage'y
ca·jole'
ca·lam'/i·ty (·ties)
cal'/ci/fi/ca'/tion
cal'/ci·fy
cal'/ci/mine
cal'/ci/na'/tion
cal/cine'
cal'/ci·um
cal'/cu/la/ble
cal'/cu/late
cal'/cu/la'/tion
cal'/cu/la'/tor
cal'/cu/lus
cal'/en/dar (schedule)
cal'/en/der (press)
calf (calves)
cal'i/ber
cal'i/brate
cal'i/bra'/tion
cal'i·co (/coes)
cal'/is/then'/ics
calk
cal/lig'/ra/phy
call'/ing
cal'/lous, *adj.*
cal'/low
cal'/lus, *n.*
calm'/ness
ca·lor'ic
cal'o/rie
cal'/um·ny (/nies)
Cal'/va·ry
Cal'/vin/ism
ca·lyp'so (/sos)
ca'ma/ra'/de/rie
cam'/ber
cam'/bric
cam'el
ca·mel'/li·a
cam'e·o (·os)
cam'/er·a
cam'i/sole
cam'/ou/flage
cam/paign'
camp'/fire'
camp'/ground'
cam'/phor
cam'/phor/at'ed

am'/pus
Ca·na'/di·an
a·nal'
an'a·pé
a·nar'y (/ies)
a·nas'ta
an'/can
an'/cel
an'/celed
an'/cel/ing
an'/cel/la'/tion
an'/cer
an'/cer/ous
an'/de/la'/brum
(/bra)
an'/did
an'/di/da·cy
an'/di/date
an'/died
an'/dle
an'dle—/foot'
an'/dle/light'
an'/dle/stick'
an'/dor
an'dy (/dies)
a'nine
an'/is/ter
an'/ker
an'/ker/ous
an'/ner
an'/ni/bal/ism
an'/ni·ly

can'/ni/ness
can'/ning
can'/non (/nons)
(gun)
can'/not
ca·noe'
ca·noe'/ing
can'on (rule)
can'o·py (/pies)
can'/ta/loupe
can/tan'/ker/ous
can/ta'ta
can/teen'
can'/ter
can'/tor
can'/vas (cloth)
can'/vass (investigate)
can'/yon
ca'pa/bil'/i·ty (·ties)
ca'pa/ble
ca·pa'/cious
ca·pac'i/tate
ca·pac'/i·ty (·ties)
ca/per
cap'/il/lar'y (/ies)
cap'i/tal (See p. 231)
cap'i/tal/ism
cap'i/tal/ist
cap'i/tal·i/za'/tion
cap'i/tal/ize
cap'i/tol (a building)
ca·pit'u/late

ca·pit′u/la′/tion
ca′pon
ca·price′
ca·pri′/cious
cap/size′
cap′/sule
cap′/tain
cap′/tain·cy
cap′/tion
cap′/ti/vate
cap′/tive
cap/tiv′/i·ty (·ties)
cap′/ture
cap′/tur/ing
ca·rafe′
car′a/mel
car′a/mel/ize
car′at (unit of weight)
car′a/van
car′a/way
car′/bide
car′/bine
car′/bo/hy′/drate
car/bol′ic
car′/bon
car′/bon/ate
car/bon′ic
car′/bon/ize
car′/bon mon/ox′/ide
Car′/bo/run′/dum
car′/bun/cle
car′/bu/ret′or
car′/cass
card′/board′
car′/di·ac
car′/di/gan
car′/di/nal
car′/di·o/gram′
car′/di·o/graph′
car′/di/ol′o·gy
ca·reen′
ca·reer′
care′/free′
care′/ful·ly
care′/less
ca·ress′
car′et (insertion mark)
care′/tak′er
care′/worn′
car′go (/goes)
car′/hop′
Ca·rib/be′an
car′i/bou, *sing. & pl.*
car′i/ca/ture
car′/il/lon
car′/load′
car′/mine
car′/nage
car′/nal
car/na′/tion
car′/ni/val
car/niv′o/rous
car′/ol/ing
ca·rouse′

ar'/pen/ter
ar'/pen/try
ar'/pet
ar'/port'
ar'/rel
ar'/riage
ar'/ri·er
ar'/rot (vegetable)
ar'/rou/sel'
ar'ry
ar'ry—/o'ver, *n.*
art'/age
arte blanche
ar/tel'
ar'/ti/lage
ar/tog'/ra/phy
ar'/ton
ar/toon'
ar/toon'/ist
ar'/tridge
as/cade'
as/car'a
ase'/ment
ase'/work'er
ash'/book'
ash'ew
ash/ier'
ash'/mere
as'/ing
a·si'no (/nos)
as'/ket
as'/pi·an

cas'/se/role
cas'/sock
cas'/ta/net'
cast'/a·way', *adj., n.*
caste
cas'/ti/gate
cas'/ti/ga'/tion
cas'/tile
cas'/tle
cast'/off'
cas'/tor
cas'u·al
cas'u/al·ty (/ties)
cat'a/clysm
cat'a/clys'/mic
cat'a/log *or* /logue
ca·tal'pa
cat'a/pult
cat'a/ract
ca·tarrh'
ca·tas'/tro/phe
cat'a/stroph'ic
catch'/all'
catch'er
catch'/word'
catch'y
cat'e/chism
cat'e/gor'/i·cal
cat'e/go'ry (/ries)
ca'ter
ca'ter—/cor'nered
ca'ter·er

cat'/er/pil'/lar
cat'/gut'
ca·thar'/sis
ca·thar'/tic
ca·the'/dral
cath'e/ter
cath'/ode
cath'o/lic
Ca·thol'i/cism
cat'/nip
cat's'—/paw', *n.*
cat'/tle
cat'/tle/man (/men)
cat'/ti/ness
cat'ty
Cau/ca'/sian
cau'/cus
cau'/li/flow'er
caus'al
cau/sa'/tion
caus'a/tive
cau'/se/rie'
cause'/way'
caus'/ing
caus'/tic
cau'/ter·i/za'/tion
cau'/ter/ize
cau'/tion
cau'/tious
cav'/al/cade
cav'a/lier'
cav'/al·ry (/ries)
cav'/al/ry/man (/men)
ca've·at emp'/tor
cav'/ern
cav'/ern/ous
cav'i·ar
cav'/i·ty (·ties)
ceased
cease'/less
ce'dar
cede (to yield)
ced'ed
ce·dil'la
ced'/ing
ceil'/ing
Cel'a/nese
cel'e/brant
cel'e/brate
cel'e/bra'/tion
ce·leb'/ri·ty (/ties)
ce·ler'/i·ty
cel'/er·y
ce·les'/tial
cel'i/ba·cy (/cies)
cel'/lar
cel'/lar·et'
cel'/list
cel'lo (/los)
cel'/lo/phane
cel'/lu/lar
Cel'/lu/loid
cel'/lu/lose
ce·ment'

cem'e/ter'y (/ies)
cen'/ser (vessel)
cen'/sor (examiner)
cen'/sor/ship
cen'/sur/a·ble
cen'/sure (blame)
cen'/sur/ing
cen'/sus
cen/ta'vo (/vos)
cen'/te/nar'i·an
cen'/te/nar'y (/ies)
cen/ten'/ni·al
cen'/ter/piece'
cen'/ti/grade
cen'/ti/gram
cen'/time
cen'/ti/me'/ter
cen'/ti/pede
cen'/tral
cen'/tral·i/za'/tion
cen'/tral/ize
cen/trif'u/gal
cen/trip'e/tal
cen/tu'/ri·on
cen'/tu·ry (/ries)
ce·phal'ic
ce·ram'/ics
ce're·al
cer'e/bel'/lum
ce·re'/bral
cer'e/bro/spi'/nal
ce·re'/brum
cer'e/mo'/ni·al
cer'e/mo'ny (/nies)
ce·rise'
cer'/tain·ly
cer'/tain·ty (/ties)
cer'/ti/fi'/a·ble
cer/tif'i/cate
cer'/ti/fi/ca'/tion
cer'/ti/fies
cer'/ti/fy'/ing
cer'/ti/tude
ce·ru'/le·an
ces/sa'/tion
ces'/sion
cess'/pool'
chafe
chaff
cha/grin'
cha/grined'
chair'/man (/men)
chaise longue
chalk'y
chal'/lenge
chal'/lis
cham'/ber
cha/me'/le·on
cham'/ois, *sing. & pl.*
cham/pagne'
cham'/pi·on
chan'/cel
chan'/cel/ler·y (/ies)
chan'/cel/lor

chan′/de/lier′
change′a/bil′/i·ty
change′/a·ble
changed
change′/less
chang′/ing
chan′/nel
chan′/neled
cha′os
cha/ot′ic
cha′/peau′ (/peaux)
chap′el
chap′/er·on
chap′/lain
chap′/ter
char′/ac/ter
char′/ac/ter/is′/tic
char′/ac/ter·i/za′/tion
char′/ac/ter/ize
cha/rade′
char′/coal′
charge′/a·ble
char′·gé′ d'af/faires′
(char′/gés′ . . .)
charg′/ing
char′i/ta/ble
char′/i·ty (·ties)
char′/la/tan
Charles′/ton, S. C.,
W. Va.
Charles′/town, Mass.
charm′/ing
charred
char′/ter
char/treuse′
chasm
chas′/sis, *sing. & pl.*
chaste
chas′/ten
chas/tise′
chas′/ti·ty
châ/teau′ (/teaus′)
Chat′/ta/noo′ga, Tenn.
chat′/tel
chat′/ter
chauf′/feur
Chau/tau′/qua, N. Y.
cheap′en
cheap′/ened
cheap′/skate′
check′/book′
check′/er/board′
check′/ered
check′/ers
check′/mate′
check′/rein′
check′up
ched′/dar
cheek′i/ness
cheer′/ful/ness
cheer′i·ly
cheer′/less
cheer′y
cheese′/cake′

cheese'/cloth'
chef
chem'/i·cal
che/mise'
chem'/ist
chem'/is/try
che/nille'
cher'/ish
Cher'o/kee'
cher'ry (/ries)
cher'ub (·u/bim)
chess'/man (/men)
ches'/ter/field
chest'/nut
chev'/ron
Chey/enne', Wyo.
chic
chick'en
chick'/en/heart'ed
chick'en pox
chic'le
chic'o·ry
chide
chief'ly
chif/fon'
chif'/fo/nier'
chig'/ger
chi'/gnon
Chi/hua'/hua
child (chil'/dren)
child'/ish
child'/less
child'/like'
chil'i con car'ne
chill'y
chim'/ney
chim'/pan/zee'
chi'/na/ware
chin/chil'la
Chi'/nese'
chintz
chip'/munk
Chip'/pen/dale
chip'/ping
chi/rog'/ra/phy
chi/rop'o/dist
chi/rop'o·dy
chi'/ro/prac'/tor
chis'el
chis'/eled
chis'/el·er
chit'/chat'
chiv'/al/rous
chiv'/al·ry
chlo'/ral
chlo'/ric
chlo'/ride
chlo'/ri/nate
chlo'/ri/na'/tion
chlo'/rine
chlo'/ro/form
chlo'/ro/phyll
choc'o/late
choir'/boy'

choke′/ber′ry (/ries)
chok′er
chol′/er · a
chol′/er · ic
choose (select)
choos′/ing
chop′/ping
chop′py
chop′/stick′
chop su′ey
cho′/ral
chord (comb. of tones)
chore
cho′/re/og′/ra/pher
cho′/re/og′/ra/phy
cho/rog′/ra/phy
cho′/rus
chose (selected)
cho′/sen
chow′/der
chow mein
chris′/ten
Chris′/ten/dom
Chris′/tian
Chris′/ti/an′/i · ty
Christ′/like′
Christ′/mas
chro/mat′ic
chro′/mi · um
chron′ic
chron′/i · cle
chro′/no/log′/i · cal
chro/nol′o · gy (/gies)
chro/nom′e/ter
chrys′a/lis
chry/san′/the/mum
chub′by
chuc′kle
chum′my
chunk′y
church′/go′er
church′/man (/men)
churl′/ish
chute
ci · ca′da (/das;/dae)
ci/der
ci · gar′
cig′a/rette′
Cin′/cin/nat′i, Ohio
cinc′/ture
cin′/der
cin′e · ma
cin′/na/mon
ci′pher
cir′/cle
cir′/cling
cir′/cuit
cir/cu′i/tous
cir′/cu/lar
cir′/cu/lar/ize
cir′/cu/late
cir′/cu/la′/tion
cir′/cu/la/to′ry
cir′/cum/cise

cir'/cum/ci'/sion
cir'/cum'/fer/ence
cir'/cum/lo/cu'/tion
cir'/cum/scribe
cir'/cum/scrip'/tion
cir'/cum/spect
cir'/cum/spec'/tion
cir'/cum/stance
cir'/cum/stan'/tial·ly
cir'/cum/stan'/ti/ate
cir'/cum/vent'
cir'/cus
cis'/tern
cit'a/del
ci·ta'/tion
cite (to quote)
cit'/ing
cit'i/zen
cit'i/zen·ry (/ries)
cit'/rate
cit'/ric
cit'/ron
cit'/rus
cit'y (/ies)
civ'/ics
civ'il
ci·vil'/ian
ci·vil'/i·ty
civ'i/li/za'/tion
civ'i/lize
civ'il·ly
claim'/ant (claimer)
clair/voy'/ant
cla'/mant (clamorous)
clam'/bake'
clam'/mi/ness
clam'my
clam'or
clam'/or/ous
clan/des'/tine
clan'/nish
clap'/board
clap'/per
claque
clar'et
clar'i/fi/ca'/tion
clar'i/fied
clar'i·fy
clar'i/net'
clar'i·on
clar'/i·ty
clas'/sic
clas'/si/cal·ly
clas'/si/cist
clas'/si/fi'/a·ble
clas'/si/fi/ca'/tion
clas'/si/fied
clas'/si·fy
class'/mate'
class'/room'
clat'/ter
clat'/tered
clause
claus'/tro/pho'/bi·a

clav'/i·cle
clean'er
clean'/li/ness
clean'/ness
cleanse
cleans'er
clear'/ance
clear'—/cut'
clear'—/eyed'
clear'/head'ed
clear'/ing/house'
cleat
cleav'/age
cleav'er
clef
cleft
clem'/en·cy (/cies)
clem'/ent
cler'gy (/gies)
cler'/gy/man
cler'ic
cler'/i·cal
Cleve'/land, Ohio
clev'er
cli/ché'
cli'/ent
cli'/en/tele'
cli'/mate
cli/mat'ic
cli'/max
climb'/ing
clinch'er
clin'ic
clin'/i·cal
cli/ni'/cian
clip'/ping
clique
cloche
clock'/wise'
clock'/work'
clois'/ter
close'/fist'ed
close'/mouthed'
close'/ness
clos'et
close'—up', *n.*
clothe, *v.*
clothes'/pin'
cloth'/ier
cloth'/ing
clot'/ted
cloud'/burst'
cloud'i/ness
clout
clo'/ver
clo'/ver/leaf' (/leaves'), *adj.*
clown'/ish/ness
club'/bing
clum'/si·ly
clum'/si/ness
clum'sy
clus'/ter
clut'/ter

coached
co·ag′u/late
co·ag′u/la′/tion
co′a/lesce′
co′a/les′/cence
co′a/li′/tion
coal mine
coarse (rough)
coars′en
coast′al
co·au′/thor
coax′/ing·ly
co·ax′i·al
co′balt
cob′/ble/stone′
co′bra
cob′/web′
co·caine′
cock′a/too′ (/toos)
cock′/eyed′
cock′i/ness
cock′/pit′
cock′/roach′
cock′/sure′
cock′/tail′
co′coa
co′co/nut′
co·coon′
cod′/dle
co′de/fend′/ant
co′deine
cod′/fish′
cod′i/cil
cod′i/fi/ca′/tion
cod′i/fied
cod′i·fy
cod′/ing
co′—ed′
co′ed′u/ca′/tion·al
co′ef/fi′/cient
co·erce′
co·er′/cion
co·er′/cive
co·ex/is′/tence
cof′/fee/pot′
cof′/fin
co′gen·cy
co′gent
cog′i/tate
co′gnac
cog′/nate
cog′/ni/zant
cog/no′/men
co·hab′it
co·hab′/it/ant
co·hab′i/ta′/tion
co·here′
co·her′/en·cy
co·her′/ent
co·he′/sion
co·he′/sive
co′hort
coif′/feur′ (hairdresser)
coif/fure′ (hairdo)

co'/in/cide'
co/in'/ci/dence
co/in'/ci/den'/tal
co'/in/sur'/ance
co'/in/sure'
co·i'/tion
coke
cold'—/blood'ed
col·i/se'um
co·li'/tis
col/lab'o/rate
col/lab'o/ra'/tion
col/lab'o/ra'/tor
col/lapse'
col/laps'/i·ble
col'/lar
col'/lar/bone'
col/late'
col/lat'/ing
col/lat'/er·al
col/la'/tor
col'/league
col/lect'
col/lect'/i·ble
col/lec'/tion
col/lec'tive
col/lec'/tiv/ism
col'/lege
col/le'/giate
col/lide'
col/li'/sion
col/lo'/qui·al
col/lu'/sion
co·logne'
co'lon
colo'/nel
co·lo'/ni·al
col'o/nist
col'o/ni/za'/tion
col'o/nize
col'/on/nade'
col'o·ny (/nies)
col'/or·a'/tion
col'o/ra/tu'ra
col'or—/blind'
col'/ored
col'/or/ful
co·los'/sal
Col'/os/se'um (Roman)
colt'/ish
col'/umn
co·lum'/nar
col'/um/nist
co'ma
com/bat'
com/bat'/ive
com'/bi/na'/tion
com/bine'
com/bus'/ti/ble
com/bus'/tion
come'/back', *n.*
co·me'/di·an, *masc.*
co·me'/di/enne', *fem.*
com'e·dy (/dies)

come'/li/ness
come'ly
com'et
com'/fort/a·ble
com'/fort·er
com'ic
com'/i·cal·ly
com'/ing
com'ma
com/mand'
com'/man/dant'
com'/man/deer'
(seize)
com/mand'er (leader)
com/mand'/ment
com/man'do (/dos)
com/mem'o/rate
com/mem'o/ra'/tion
com/mence'/ment
com/mend'/a·ble
com'/men/da'/tion
com/men'/su/ra/bil'-
/i·ty
com/men'/su/ra/ble
com/men'/su/rate·ly
com'/ment
com'/men/tar'y (/ies)
com'/men/ta'/tor
com'/merce
com/mer'/cial
com/mer'/cial/ism
com/mer'/cial/ize
com/mis'/er/ate
com/mis'/er·a'/tion
com'/mis/sar'
com'/mis/sar'i·at
com'/mis/sar'y (/ies)
com/mis'/sion
com/mis'/sion·er
com/mit'/ment
com/mit'/ted
com/mit'/tee
com/mit'/tee/man
(/men)
com/mode'
com/mo'/di/ous
com/mod'/i·ty (·ties)
com'/mo/dore'
com'/mon
com'/mon/place'
com'/mon/wealth'
com/mo'/tion
com'/mu/nal
com/mune'
com/mu'/ni/ca/ble
com/mu'/ni/cant
com/mu'/ni/cate
com/mu'/ni/ca'/tion
com/mu'/ni/ca'/tive
com/mu'/nion
com/mu'/ni/qué
com'/mu/nism
com'/mu/nis'/tic
com/mu'/ni·ty (/ties)

com/mut'/a · ble
com'/mu/ta'/tion
com/mute'
com/mut'er
com/pact', *adj.*
com/pan'/ion/a · ble
com/pan'/ion/ship
com'/pa · ny (/nies)
com'/pa/ra/ble
com'/pa/ra/bil'/i · ty
com/par'a/tive
com/pare'
com/par'i/son
com/part'/ment
com'/pass
com/pas'/sion
com/pas'/sion/ate · ly
com/pat'i/bil'/i · ty
com/pat'/i · ble
com/pa'/tri · ot
com/pel'
com/pelled'
com/pel'/ling
com/pen'/di · um
(/ums; /di · a)
com/pen'/sa/ble
com'/pen/sate
com'/pen/sa'/tion
com/pen'/sa/to'ry
com/pete'
com'/pe/tence
com'/pe/tent · ly
com'/pe/ti'/tion
com/pet'i/tive
com/pet'i/tor
com'/pi/la'/tion
com/pile'
com/pla'/cen · cy
(/cies)
com/pla'/cent
com/plain'
com/plain'/ant
com/plaint'
com/plai'/sant
com'/ple/ment (fill up)
com'/ple/men'/ta · ry
com/plete'
com/ple'/tion
com/plex'
com/plex'/ion
com/plex'/i · ty (· ties)
com/pli'/ance
com'/pli/cate
com'/pli/ca'/tion
com/plic'/i · ty (· ties)
com/plied'
com'/pli/ment (flatter)
com'/pli/men'/ta · ry
com/ply'
com/po'/nent
com/pose'
com/pos'/ed · ly
com/pos'er
com/pos'/ite

com′/po/si′/tion
com/pos′i/tor
com/po′/sure
com′/pound, *n. & adj.*
com/pound′, *v.*
com′/pre/hend′
com′/pre/hend′/i·ble
com′/pre/hen′/si/ble
com′/pre/hen′/sion
com/press′, *v.*
com′/press, *n.*
com/press′/i·ble
com/pres′/sion
com/pres′/sor
com/prise′
com′/pro/mise
Comp/tom′e/ter
comp/trol′/ler
com/pul′/sion
com/pul′/so·ry
com/punc′/tion
com/put′/a·ble
com′/pu/ta′/tion
com/pute′
com/put′er
com′/rade
con′/cave
con/ceal′/ment
con/cede′
con/ced′ed
con/ceit′
con/ceiv′/a·bly
con/ceive′
con′/cen/trate
con′/cen/tra′/tion
con/cen′/tric
con′/cept
con/cep′/tion
con/cep′/tu·al
con′/cert, *n. & adj.*
con/cert′, *v.*
con/cer′to (/tos)
con/ces′/sion
con/ces′/sion/aire′
con/cil′i/ate
con/cil′i/a′tion
con/cil′i/a·to′ry
con/cise′
con′/clave
con/clude′
con/clu′/sion
con/coct′
con/coc′/tion
con/com′i/tant
con′/cord
con/cor′/dance
con′/course
con′/crete, *n.*
con/cur′
con/curred′
con/cur′/rence
con/cus′/sion
con/demn′
con′/dem/na′/tion

con′/den/sa′/tion
con/dense′
con/dens′er
con′/de/scend′
con′de/scen′/sion
con′/di/ment
con/di′/tion · al
con/di′/tioned
con/dole′
con/do′/lence
con/done′
con/duce′
con/du′/cive
con/duct′, *v.*
con′/duct, *n.*
con/duc′/tance
con/duc′/tor
con′/duit
con/fec′/tion
con/fec′/tion/er′y (/ies)
con/fed′/er · a · cy (/cies)
con/fed′/er/ate
con/fer′
con′/fer · ee′
con′/fer/ence
con/ferred′
con/fer′/ring
con/fess′
con/fes′/sion
con/fes′/sion · al
con/fes′/sor
con′/fi/dant, *masc.*
con′/fi/dante, *fem.*
con′/fi/dence
con′/fi/den′/tial · ly
con/fig′u/ra′/tion
con/fine′, *v.* (restrict)
con/fine′/ment
con′/fines, *n. pl.* (boundary)
con/firm′
con′/fir/ma′/tion
con/′/fis/cate
con′/fis/ca′/tion
con/fis′/ca/to′ry
con′/fla/gra′/tion
con/flict′, *v.*
con′/flict, *n.*
con/form′
con/form′/a · ble
con/form′/ist
con/for′/mi · ty (/ties)
con/found′
con/found′ed
con/front′
con/fuse′
con/fu′/sion
con′/fu/ta′/tion
con/fute′
con′ga
con/geal′
con/ge′/nial

con/ge′/ni/al′/i·ty
con/gen′i/tal
con/gest′
con/ges′/tion
con/glom′/er/ate
con/glom′/er·a′/tion
con/grat′u/late
con/grat′u/la′/tions
con/grat′u/la/to′ry
con′/gre/gate
con′/gre/ga′/tion·al
con′/gress
con/gres′/sion·al
con′/gress/man (/men)
con/gru′/i·ty (·ties)
con′/gru/ous
con′ic
con′/i·cal
co′ni/fer
co·nif′/er/ous
con/jec′/tur·al
con/jec′/ture
con′/ju/gate
con′/ju/ga′/tion
con/junc′/tion
con′/jure
con′/jur·er
con/nect′
Con/nect′i/cut
con/nec′/tion
con/nip′/tion
con/niv′/ance
con/nive′
con′/nois/seur′
con′/no/ta′/tion
con/note′
con′/quer/ing
con′/quer·or
con′/quest
con′/science
con′/sci/en′/tious
con′/scious/ness
con′/script, *n. & adj.*
con/scrip′/tion
con′/se/crate
con′/se/cra′/tion
con/sec′u/tive
con/sen′/sus (/sus·es)
con/sent′
con′/se/quence
con′/se/quen′/tial
con′/ser/va′/tion
con/ser′/va/tive
con/ser′/va/to·ry(/ries)
con/serve′
con/sid′er
con/sid′/er/a·ble
con/sid′/er/ate
con/sid′/er·a′/tion
con/sid′/ered
con/sign′
con′/sign·ee′
con/sign′/ment
con/sign′or

con/sist'
con/sis'/ten·cy (/cies)
con/sis'/tent
con'/so/la'/tion
con/sole'
con/sol'i/date
con/sol'i/da'/tion
con'/som·mé'
con'/so/nant
con'/sort, *n.*
con/sort', *v.*
con/spic'u/ous
con/spir'a·cy (/cies)
con/spir'a/tor
con/spire'
con'/sta/ble
con'/stan·cy
con'/stant
con'/stel/la'/tion
con'/ster/na'/tion
con'/sti/pate
con'/sti/pa'/tion
con/stit'u/en·cy (/cies)
con/stit'u/ent
con'/sti/tute
con'/sti/tu'/tion·al
con'/sti/tu'/tion/al'/i·ty (·ties)
con'/sti/tu'/tion/al·ly
con/strain'
con/straint'
con/strict'
con/struct'
con/struc'/tion
con/struc'/tive
con/strue'
con/stru'/ing
con'/sul (govt. official)
con'/su/lar
con'/su/late
con/sult'
con/sul'/tant
con'/sul/ta'/tion
con/sum'/a·ble
con/sume'
con/sum'/mate, *adj.*
con'/sum/mate, *v.*
con'/sum/ma'/tion
con/sump'/tion
con/sump'/tive
con'/tact
con/ta'/gious
con/tain'er
con/tam'i/nate
con/tam'i/na'/tion
con'/tem/plate
con'/tem/pla'/tion
con/tem'/po/ra'/ne/ous
con/tem'/po/rar'y (/ies)
con/tempt'
con/tempt'/i·ble

con/temp'/tu/ous
con/tend'
con'/tent (that which is contained)
con/tent' (satisfied)
con/ten'/tion
con/ten'/tious
con/test', *v.*
con'/test, *n.*
con/test'/a·ble
con/tes'/tant
con'/text
con/tex'/tu·al
con'/ti/gu'/i·ty
con/tig'u/ous
con'/ti/nent
con'/ti/nen'/tal
con/tin'/gen·cy (/cies)
con/tin'/gent
con/tin'u·al
con/tin'u/ance
con/tin'u/a'tion
con/tin'·ue
con/tin'u/ing
con'/ti/nu'/i·ty (·ties)
con/tin'u/ous
con/tort'
con/tor'/tion/ist
con'/tour
con'/tra/band
con'/tract, *n.*
con/tract', *v.*
con/trac'/tion
con/trac'/tor
con/trac'/tu·al
con'/tra/dict'
con'/tra/dic'/tion
con'/tra/dic'/to·ry
con'/tra/dis/tinc'/tion
con'/tra/in'/di/cate
con/tral'to (/tos)
con'/tra/ri/wise'
con'/tra·ry
con/trast'
con'/tra/vene'
con'/tra/ven'/tion
con'/tre/temps'
con/trib'/ute
con'/tri/bu'/tion
con/trib'u/tor
con/trib'u/to'ry
con'/trite
con/tri'/tion
con/triv'/ance
con/trive'
con/trol'
con/trolled'
con/trol'/ler
con'/tro/ver'/sial
con'/tro/ver'sy (/sies)
con'/tro/vert
con/tuse'

con/tu′/sion
co·nun′/drum
con′/va/les′/cence
con′/va/lesc′/ing
con/vec′/tion
con/vene′
con/ve′/nience
con′/vent
con/ven′/tion
con/ven′/tion/al′/i·ty (·ties)
con/verge′
con/ver′/gence
con/ver′/sant
con′/ver/sa′/tion
con′/ver/sa′/tion/al/ist
con/verse′, *v.*
con′/verse, *n. & adj.*
con/ver′/sion
con/vert′, *v.*
con′/vert, *n.*
con/vert′/i·ble
con′/vex
con/vey′
con/vey′/ance
con/vey′er
con′/vict, *n.*
con/vict′, *v.*
con/vic′/tion
con/vince′
con/vinc′/ing·ly
con/viv′i·al
con/viv′i/al′/i·ty (·ties)
con′/vo/ca′/tion
con/voke′
con′/vo/lu′/tion
con′/voy, *n.*
con/voy′, *v.*
con/voyed′
con/vulse′
con/vul′/sion
cook′/book′
cook′er
cool′er
coo′/lie (laborer)
cool′ly (calmly)
co·op′/er/ate
co·op′/er·a′/tion
co·or′/di/nate
co′pi/ous
cop′/per
cop′ra
cop′u/la′/tive
cop′y/hold′er
cop′y/right′
cop′y/writ′er
co′quet·ry
co·quette′
cor′al
cord′/age
cor′/dial
cor/dial′/i·ty (·ties)
cor′/don

cor'/du/roy
co·re/spon'/dent
(third party in divorce)
cor'/nea
cor'/ner
cor'/ner/stone'
cor/net'
cor'/nice
cor/nu/co'/pia
cor'/ol/lar'y (/ies)
cor'o/nar'y
cor'o/na'/tion
cor'o/ner
cor·o/net'
cor'/po/ral
cor'/po/rate
cor'/po/ra'/tion
cor/po'/re·al
corps, *sing. & pl.*
corpse
corps'/man
cor'/pu/lence
cor'/pus (/po·ra)
cor'/pus/cle
cor/ral'
cor/rect'
cor/rec'/tion
cor'/re/late
cor'/re/la'/tion
cor/rel'a/tive
cor'/re/spond'
cor'/re/spon'/dence
cor'/ri/dor
cor/rob'o/rate
cor/rob'o/ra'/tion
cor/rode'
cor/ro'/sion
cor'/ru/gate
cor'/ru/ga'/tion
cor/rupt'
cor/rupt'/i·ble
cor/rup'/tion
cor/sage'
cor/tege'
cor'/ti/sone
cos/met'ic
cos'/me/tol'o/gist
cos'/me/tol'o·gy
cos'/mic
cos'/mo/naut
cos'/mo/pol'i/tan
cos'/mos
cost'/li/ness
cos'/tume
cos'/tum·er
cot'/tage
cot'/ton
coun'/cil
(governing body)
coun'/cil/man (/men)
coun'/cil/lor
coun'/sel (advice)
coun'/sel/or
coun'/te/nance

coun′/ter/act′
coun′/ter/bal′/ance
coun′/ter/claim′
coun′/ter/clock′/wise′
coun′/ter/feit
coun′/ter/mand′
coun′/ter/part′
coun′/ter/point′
coun′/ter/sign′
count′/ess
count′/less
coun′/tri/fied
coun′/try (/tries)
coun′/try/man (/men)
coun′/try/side′
coun′ty (/ties)
coup d'é•tat′
cou′pé′
cou′/ple
cou′/pling
cou′/pon
cour′/age
cou/ra′/geous•ly
cou′/ri•er
course (direction)
cour′/te/ous
cour′/te•sy (/sies)
court′/house′
court′—/mar′tial
(courts— . . .)
court′/room′
court′/ship
cous′in
cov′e/nant
cov′/er/age
cov′/ered
co′•vert
cov′/et/ous
cov′ey
cow′/ard
cow′/ard/ice
cow′/boy′
cow′er
co—/work′er
coy′ly
co′zy
co′zi•ly
crack′er
crack′le
crack′—up′, *n.*
cra′/dle
craft′i•ly
crafts′/man (/men)
crammed
cran′/ber′ry (/ries)
cra′/ni•al
cra/ni/ol′o•gy
cra′/ni•um
(/ums; /ni•a)
crank′i/ness
crank′y
cran′ny (/nies)
cra′/ter
cra/vat′

crav'/ing
cray'on
cra'/zi·ly
cra'/zi/ness
cra'zy
cream'/er·y (/ies)
cre/ate'
cre·a'/tion
cre·a'/tor
crea'/ture
cre'/dence
cre/den'/tial
cred'i/bil'/i·ty
cred'/i·ble
cred'it
cred'/it/a·ble
cred'i/tor
cre'do (/dos)
cre/du'/li·ty (/ties)
cred'u/lous
creep'y
creep'i/ness
cre'/mate
cre/ma'/tion
cre'/ma/to'ry (/ries)
cre'/ole
cre'o/sote
crepe
cre/scen'do (/dos)
cres'/cent
crest'ed
crest'/fall'en
cre/tonne'
cre/vasse'
crev'/ice
crick'et
cried
crim'i/nal
crim'i/nol'o·gy
crim'/son
cringe
crin'/kle
crin'o/line
crip'/ple
crip'/pling
cri'/sis (/ses)
crisp'ly
criss'/cross'
cri/te'/ri·on (/ri·a)
crit'ic
crit'/i·cal
crit'i/cism
crit'i/cize
cri/tique'
crook'/ed/ness
cro/quet'
cro/quette'
cross'—/ex·am'i·na'tion
cross'—/ex·am'ine
cross'—/eyed'
cross in'dex, *n.*
(·dex·es; di/ces)
cross—/in'·dex, *v.*
cross'/o'ver, *n.*

cross'—/ques'tion
cross ref'/er/ence, *n.*
cross'—/ref'er • ence
crowd'ed
crowned
cru'/cial
cru'/ci/fied
cru'/ci/fix
cru'/ci/fix'/ion
cru'/ci • fy
crude'/ness
cru'/di/ty (/ties)
cru'el
cru'/el • ty (/ties)
cruis'er
crum'/ble
crum'/bling
crum'/ple
crum'/pling
crunched
crunch'/ing
cru/sade'
crust'i/ness
crux
cry'/ing
crypt
cryp'/tic
crys'/tal
cryst'/tal/line
cryst'/tal/li/za'/tion
crys'/tal/lize
cub'/by/hole'
cu'bic
cu'bi/cal, *adj.*
cu'bi/cle, *n.*
cud'/dle
cui/sine'
cu'li/nar'y
cul'/mi/nate
cul'/mi/na'/tion
cu • lottes', *pl.*
cul'/pa/bil'/i • ty
cul'/pa/ble
cul'/prit
cul'/ti/vate
cul'/ti/va'/tion
cul'/tur • al
cul'/ture
cum'/ber/some
cum'/brous
cum lau'de
cu'mu/late
cu' • mu/la'/tive
cun'/ning • ly
cup'/board
cup'/ful (/fuls)
cu • pid'/i • ty
cu'po • la
cupped
cups full
cur'/a • ble
cu'rate
cu • ra'/tor
curb'/ing

ur'/dle
ure'—/all'
ur'/few
u'ri·o (·os)
u'ri/os'/i·ty (·ties)
u'ri/ous·ly
url'i/ness
ur'/rant (berry)
ur'/ren·cy (/cies)
ur'/rent (prevailing)
ur/ric'u/lum
(/lums; ·u·la)
ur'/ried
ur'ry
ur'/sive
ur'/so·ry
ur/tail'
ur'/tain
ur/va'/ceous
ur'/va/ture
urv'/ing
cush'/ion
cus'/tard
cus/to'/di·an
cus'/to·dy (/dies)
cus'/tom
cus'/tom/ar'y
cus'/tom/ar'i·ly
cus'/tom·er (/ers)
cu·ta'/ne/ous
cut'/a·way'
cu'ti/cle
cut'/ler·y
cut'/let
cut'—/rate', *adj.*
cut'/throat'
cy'an/ide
cy'cle
cy'clic
cy'clone
cy'clo/pe'/di·a
cy'clo/tron
cyl'/in/der
cy·lin'/dri/cal
cym'/bal
cyn'ic
cyn'/i·cal
cyn'i/cism
cy'no/sure
cy'press
cyst
czar
Czech
Czecho/slo/va'/kia

D

dab'/ble
Da'cron
daf'/fo/dil
dai'ly (/lies)
dain'/ti/ness
dain'ty
dair'y (/ies)
dair'y/ing
da'is
dai'sy (/sies)
dal'/li/ance
dal'ly
dam'/age
dam'/ask
dammed (blocked)
dam'/ming
damned (cursed)
damp'en
danc'/ing
dan'/der
dan'dy
dan'/ger/ous
dan'/gle
Dan'/ish
dap'/per
dare'/dev'il
dar'/ing·ly
dark'en
dark'/ness
dark'/room'
dar'/ling
dash'/board'
das'/tard·ly
dat'ed
da'tum (da'ta)
daubed
daugh'/ter
daugh'ter—/in—/law'
(daugh'ters— . . .)
daunt'/less·ly
dav'/en/port
dawned
day'/break'
day'/dream'
day' let'/ter
day'/light'
day'/time'
daz'/ed·ly
daz'/zle
dea'/con
dead'/en/ing
dead'/line
dead'/li/ness
dead'/lock'

eaf'/en/ing·ly
earth
eath'ly
e·ba'/cle
e'bar/ka'/tion
e·base'
e·bat'/a·ble
e·bate'
e·ben'/ture
e·bil'i/tate
eb'it
eb'o/nair'
e·bris'
ebt'or
e'but
eb'u/tante
ec'/ade
ec'a/dent
e'cal
e·cant'er
e·cayed'
e·cease' (death)
e·ce'/dent
e·ceit'/ful·ly
e·ceive'
e'cen·cy (/cies)
e'cent
e·cen'/tral/ize
e·cep'/tion
e·cep'/tive
ec'·i/bel
e·cide'

de·cid'/ed·ly
de·cid'u/ous
dec'i/mal
de·ci'/pher/a·ble
de·ci'/sion
de·claim'
dec'/la/ma'/tion
de·clam'a/to·ry
dec'/la/ra'/tion
de·clar'a/tive
de·clare'
de·clen'/sion
de·cline'
dé'col'/le·té'
de'com/pose'
de'com/po/si'/tion
dé'cor'
dec'o/rate
dec'o/ra'/tion
dec'o/rous
de·co'/rum
de'crease, *n.*
de·crease', *v.*
de·cree'
de·crep'it
ded'i/cate
ded'i/ca'/tion
de·duc'/i·ble
de·duct'/i·ble
de·duc'/tion
deep'en
deep'/freeze'

de•face′
de fac′to
def′a/ma′/tion
de•fam′a/to′ry
de•fame′
de•fault′
de•feat′/ism
de•fect′
de•fec′/tive
de•fend′
de•fen′/dant
de•fense′
de•fen′/si/ble
de•fen′/sive
de•fer′
def′/er/ence
def′/er/en′/tial
(polite)
de•ferred′
de•fer′/ring
de•fi′/ance
de•fi′/cien•cy (/cies)
def′i/cit
de•fied′
de•file′/ment
de•fin′/a•ble
de•fine′
def′i/nite
def′i/ni′/tion
de•fin′i/tive
de•flate′
de•flect′
de•flec′/tion
de•form′/i•ty (•ties)
de•fraud′
de•frayed′
de•frost′er
deft′ly
de•funct′
de•fy′/ing
de•gen′/er•a•cy
de•gen′/er/ate
deg′/ra/da′/tion
de•grade′
de•gree′
de′hu/mid′i•fy
de•hy′/drate
deign
de′i•ty (•ties)
de•ject′/ed•ly
de•jec′/tion
de ju′re
Del′a/ware
de•layed′
de•lec′/ta/ble
del′e/gate
del′e/ga′/tion
de•lete′
del′e/te′/ri/ous
de•le′/tion
de•lib′/er/ate
de•lib′/er•a′/tion
del′i/ca•cy (/cies)
del′i/cate

el'i/ca/tes'/sen
e·li'/cious
e·light'/ful·ly
e·lim'it
e·lim'i/ta'/tion
e·lin'e/ate
e·lin'e/a'tion
e·lin'/quen·cy
(/cies)
e·lir'i/ous
e·lir'i·um tre'/mens
e·liv'er
e·liv'/er·y (/ies)
el'ta
e·lude'
el'/uge
e·lu'/sion
e·luxe'
e·mag'/ne/tize
em'a/gogue
e·mand'
e'mar/ca'/tion
e·mean'or
e·ment'ed
e·men'/ti·a prae'-
/cox
e·mer'it
e·mise'
em'i/tasse'
e·mo'/bi/li/za'/tion
e·moc'/ra·cy (/cies)
em'o/crat'ic

dem'o/crat'/i·cal·ly
de·mol'/ish
dem'o/li'/tion
de'mon
de·mon'e/tize
dem'/on/strate
dem'/on/stra'/tion
de·mon'/stra/tive
de·mor'/al/ize
de·mur' (delay)
de·mure' (modest)
de·mur'/rage
de·murred'
de·na'/tured
de·ni'al
de·nies'
den'im
de·nom'i/na'/tion
de·note'
de·noue'/ment
de·nounce'
den'/si·ty (/ties)
den'/tal
den'/ti/frice
den'/tin
den'tist·ry
den'/ture
de·nun'/ci·a'/tion
de·ny'
de·o'/dor/ant
de·part'/ment
de·part/men'/tal

de·par′/ture
de·pend′/a·ble
de·pend′a/bil′/i·ty
de·pen′/dent
de·pict′
de·pic′/tion
de·pil′a/to′·ry (/ries)
de·plete′
de·ple′/tion
de·plor′/a·ble
de·plore′
de·ploy′
de′por/ta′/tion
de·port′/ment
de·pose′
de·pos′it
de·pos′i/tar′y (/ies)
dep′o/si′/tion
de·pos′i/tor
de·pos′i/to′ry (/ries)
de′pot
dep′/ra/va′/tion
(corruption)
de·prave′
de·prav′/i·ty (·ties)
dep′/re/cate
dep′/re/ca′/tion
de·pre′/ci/ate
de·pre′/ci·a′/tion
dep′/re/da′/tion
de·pressed′
de·pres′/sion
dep′/ri/va′/tion (loss
de·prive′
dep′u/tize
dep′u·ty (/ties)
de·rail′
de·ranged′
der′e/lict
de·ride′
de·ri′/sion
der′i/va′/tion
de·riv′a/tive
de·rive′
der′/ma/tol′o·gy
de·rog′a/to′ry
der′/rick
de·scend′
de·scen′/dant
de·scent′
de·scrib′/a·ble
de·scribe′
de·scrip′/tion
des′e/crate
des′e/cra′/tion
de′seg/re/ga′/tion
de·sen′/si/tize
des′/ert, *n.*
(dry country)
de·sert′, *v.* (to leave)
de·ser′/tion
de·serve′
de·serv′/ed·ly
des′/ic/cate

es'/ic/ca'/tion
e · sign'
es'/ig/nate
es'/ig/na'/tion
e · sign'er
e · sir'a/bil'/i · ty
e · sir'/a · ble
e · sire'
e · sir'/ous
e · sist'
es Moines', Iowa
es'o/late
es'o/la'/tion
e · spair'
es'/per/ate
es'/per · a'/tion
e · spi'/ca/ble
e · spise'
e · spite'
e · spon'/den · cy
es'/pot
es'/po/tism
es/sert' (food)
es'/ti/na'/tion
es'/tined
es'/ti · ny (/nies)
es'/ti/tute
e · stroy'
e · struc'/ti/ble
e · struc'/tion
es'/ul/to'ry
e · tach'/a · ble

de · tach'/ment
de · tailed'
de · tain'
de · tect'
de · tec'/tive
de · ten'/tion
de · ter'
de · ter'/gent
de · te'/ri · o/rate
de · te'/ri · o/ra'/tion
de · ter'/mi/na/ble
de · ter'/mi/na'/tion
de · ter'/mine
de · ter'/min/ism
de · terred'
de · ter'/rent
de · test'/a · ble
det'o/nate
det'o/na'/tor
de'tour
de · tract'
de · trac'/tion
det'/ri/ment
det'/ri/men'/tal
de · val'u/ate
dev'/as/ta'/tion
de · vel'op
de · vel'/op/ment
de·vel'/oped
de'vi/ate
de'vi · a'/tion
de · vice', *n.*

dev′/il/ish
de′vi/ous
de·vis′/a·ble
(given by will)
de·vise′, *v.*
de·vi′/tal/ize
de·void′
de·volve′
de·vote′
de·vot′/ed·ly
de·vo′/tion
de·vour′
de·vout′
dex/ter′/i·ty
dex′/ter/ous
dex′/trose
di′a/be′/tes
di′a/bet′ic
di′a/bol′ic
di′a/bol′/i·cal
di′ag/nose
di′ag/no′/sis (/ses)
di′ag/nos′/tic
di′ag/nos/ti′/cian
di·ag′o/nal
di′a/gram
di′al
di′a/lect
di′aled
di′a/logue
di·am′e/ter
di′a/mond
di′a/per
di′a/phragm
di′ar/rhe′a
di′a·ry (/ries)
di′a/ther′my
di·chot′o·my
Dic′/ta/phone
dic′/tate
dic/ta′/tion
dic′/ta/to′/ri·al
dic′/tion
dic′/tio/nary (/ies)
Dic′/to/graph
dic′/tum (·ta)
di·dac′/tic
died (perished)
die′/sel
di′et
di′e/tet′/ics
di′e/ti′/tian
dif′/fer/ence
dif′/fer/en′/tial
(pert. to difference)
dif′/fer/en′/ti/ate
dif′/fer/en′/ti·a′/tion
dif′/fi/cult
dif′/fi/cul·ty (/ties)
dif′/fi/dence
dif/frac′/tion
dif/fuse′
dif/fu′/sion
di′gest, *n.*

li·gest′, *v.*
li·gest′/i·ble
li·ges′/tion
lig′/ging
lig′it
lig′/it·al com/put′er
lig′i/tal′is
lig′/ni/fied
lig′/ni·fy
lig′/ni/tar′y (/ies)
lig′/ni·ty
li·gress′
li·gres′/sion
li·lap′i/dat′ed
li·late′
lil′a/to′ry
li·lem′ma
lil′i/gence
li·lute′
li·lu′/tion
li·men′/sion·al
li·min′/ish
li·min′u/tive
lim′i·ty (·ties)
limmed
lim′/ness
lim′/ple
lin′er
li·nette′
lin′/ghy (/ghies)
(boat)
lin′/gi/ness
din′gy (grimy)
din′/ner
di·oc′e/san
di′o/cese (/ceses)
di·ox′/ide
diph/the′/ri·a
diph′/thong
di·plo′ma
di·plo′/ma·cy (/cies)
dip′/lo/mat
di·rect′
di·rec′/tion
di·rec′/tive
di·rec′/tor
di·rec′/to/rate
di·rec′/to·ry (/ries)
dire′ly
dir′i/gi/ble
dirt′i/ness
dirt′y
dis/a·bil′/i·ty
dis/a′bled
dis′/ad/van′/tage
dis/ad′/van/ta′-
/geous·ly
dis′/af/fect′ed
dis′/af/firm′
dis′/a·gree′/a·ble
dis′/a·gree′/ment
dis′/al/low′
dis′/ap/pear′
dis′/ap/pear′/ance

dis'/ap/point'
dis'/ap/pro/ba'/tion
dis'/ap/prov'al
dis'/ap/prove'
dis/ar'/ma/ment
dis/arm'/ing
dis'/ar/range'
dis'/ar/ray'
dis'/as/so'/ci/ate
di·sas'/ter
dis/as'/trous
dis'/a·vow'al
dis/band'
dis/bar'
dis/bar'/ring
dis'/be/lief'
dis'/be/liev'er
dis/burse'/ment
dis/burs'/ing
dis/card', *v.*
dis'/card, *n.*
dis/cern'
dis/cern'/i·ble
dis/charge'
dis/ci'/ple
dis'/ci/pli/nar'·i·an
dis'/ci/pline
dis/claim'
dis/close'
dis/clo'/sure
dis/col'or
dis/col'/or·a'/tion
dis/com'/fi/ture
(frustration)
dis/com'/fort
dis'/com/mode'
dis'/com/pose'
dis'/com/po'/sure
dis'/con/cert'
dis'/con/nect'
dis/con'/so/late
dis'/con/tent'
dis'/con/tin'ue
dis'/cord, *n.*
dis/cord', *v.*
dis/cor'/dant
dis'/count
dis/cour'/age/ment
dis/course'
dis/cour'/te/ous
dis/cov'/er·y (/ies)
dis/cred'/it/a·ble
dis/creet'
dis/crep'/an·cy (/cies)
dis/cre'/tion
dis/cre'/tion/ar'y
dis/crim'i/nate
dis/crim'i/na'/tion
dis/cur'/sive
dis/cuss'
dis/cus'/sion
dis/dain'
dis/ease' (illness)
dis/em'/bar/ka'/tion

dis'/en/chant'/ment
dis'/en/gage'
dis/fa'/vor
dis/fig'/ured
dis/fran'/chise
dis/gorge'
dis/grace'/ful
dis/grun'/tle
dis/guise'
dis/gust'
dis/heart'/ened
dis/hon'/est
dis/hon'/es · ty
dis/hon'/or/a · ble
dis'/il/lu'/sion
dis'/in/clined'
dis'/in/fect'
dis/in/fec'/tant
dis'/in/her'it
dis/in'/te/grate
dis/in'/ter/est · ed
dis/joint'ed
dis/like'
dis'/lo/cate
dis/lodge'
dis/loy'/al · ty
dis'/mal
dis/man'/tle
dis/man'/tling
dis/may'
dis/miss'al
dis/mount'

dis'/o · be'/di/ence
dis'/o · beyed'
dis'/o · blig'/ing
dis/or'/der · ly
dis/or'/der/li/ness
dis/or'/gan · i/za'/tion
dis/or'/gan/ize
dis/own'
dis/par'/ag/ing · ly
dis'/pa/rate
dis/par'/i · ty (· ties)
dis/pas'/sion/ate
dis/patch'
dis/pel'
dis/pelled'
dis/pel'/ling
dis/pen'/sa/ble
dis/pen'/sa · ry (/ries)
dis/pen/sa'/tion
dis/pense'
dis/per'/sal, *n.*
dis/perse'
dis/pir'/it · ed
dis/placed'
dis/play'
dis/please'
dis/plea'/sure
dis/pos'al
dis/pose'
dis'/po/si'/tion
dis'/pos/sess'
dis'/pro/por'/tion/ate

dis/prove'
dis/pute'
dis/qual'i/fied
dis/qual'i·fy
dis/qui'/et/ing
dis'/re/gard'
dis'/re/pair'
dis/rep'u/ta/ble
dis'/re/pute'
dis'/re/spect'/ful
dis/robe'
dis/rupt'
dis'/sat/is/fac'/tion
dis/sat'/is/fied
dis/sat'/is·fy
dis/sect'
dis/sec'/tion
dis/sem'/ble
dis/sem'i/nate
dis/sen'/sion
dis/sent'
dis'/ser/ta'/tion
dis/ser'/vice
dis/sim'i/lar
dis/sim'i/lar'/i·ty
(·ties)
dis/sim'i/la'/tion
dis/sim'u/late
dis'/si/pate
dis'/si/pa'/tion
dis/sol'u/ble
dis'/so/lute
dis'/so/lu'/tion
dis/solve'
dis/solv'/ing
dis'/so/nance
dis/suade'
dis/sua'/sion
dis'/tance
dis/taste'/ful
dis/tem'/per
dis/tend'
dis/ten'/tion
dis/till'
dis'/til/la'/tion
dis/tinct'
dis/tinc'/tion
dis/tin'/guish
dis/tort'
dis/tor'/tion
dis/tract'
dis/trac'/tion
dis/traught'
dis/tress'
dis/trib'/ute
dis'/tri/bu'/tion
dis/trib'u/tor
dis'/trict
dis/trust'/ful
dis/tur'/bance
dis/use'
dit'to (/tos)
di'van
di·verge'

di · ver'/gence
di · verse' (various)
di · ver'/si/fi/ca'/tion
di · ver'/si/fied
di · ver'/si · fy
di · ver'/sion
di · ver'/si · ty (/ties)
di · vert'
di · vest'
di · vide'
div'i/dend
div'i/na'/tion
di · vine'
di · vin'/i · ty (· ties)
di · vis'i/bil'/i · ty
di · vis'/i · ble
(capable of being separated)
di · vi'/sion
di · vi'/sor
di · vorce'
di · vor'cé', *masc.*
di · vor'/cée', *fem.*
di · vulge'
diz'/zi/ness
diz'zy
doc'/ile
do · cil'/i · ty
dock'et
doc'/tor
doc'/tor · al
doc'/tor/ate
doc'/tri/nal
doc'/trine
doc'u/ment
doc'u/men/ta'/tion
dodg'er
doe'/skin'
dog'/ged/ness
dog'/ger · el
dog'ma
dog/mat'ic
dog'/ma/tism
dog'—/tired'
dog'/wood'
dole'/ful
dol'/lar
dol'/or/ous
do · main'
do · mes'/tic
do · mes'/ti/cat · ed
do'mes/tic'/i · ty
dom'i/cile
dom'i/nance
dom'i/na'/tion
dom'i/neer'/ing
Do · min'i/can
do · min'/ion
dom'i · no (/noes)
do'nate
do · na'/tion
do'nor
doo'/dle
door'/nail'

door'/step'
door'/way'
door'/yard'
dor'/mant
dor'/mer
dor'/mi/to'ry (/ries)
dos'/age
dos'/si·er
dot'/age
dot'/ing
dou'/ble
dou'ble—/breast'ed
dou/ble/head'er
dou·ble—/park'
dou·ble—/quick'
dou'ble—/talk
dou'ble—/time, *v.*
doubt'/ful
doubt'/less
dough'/nut'
dove'/tail'
dow'a/ger
dow'dy
dow'/di/ness
down'/cast'
down'/fall'
down'/grade'
down'/heart'ed
down'/hill'
down'/pour'
down'/right'
down'/stairs', *adv., adj.*
down'/stairs', *n.*
down'/town'
down'/trod'/den
down'/ward
dox/ol'o·gy (/gies)
doz'en
drafts'/man
draft'y
dragged
drag'/ging
drag'/net
drain'/age
drain'/pipe'
dra'ma
dra/mat'ic
dra'/ma/tize'
drap'/er·y
dras'/tic
dras'/ti/cal·ly
draw'/back'
draw'ee'
draw'er
dray'/age
dread'/ful
dread'/nought'
dream'i·ly
dream'i/ness
drear'i·ly
drear'y
dredged
dress'er
dress'/mak'er

drib'/ble
dri'er
drilled
drink'/a·ble
drip
dripped
drip'/ping
drive'—in', *n.*
driv'el
driv'er
drive'/way'
driz'/zle
droop'y
dropped
drop'/ping
drought
drow'sy
drow'/si/ness
drudg'/er·y (/ies)
drugged
drug'/gist
drug'/store'
drummed
drum'/mer
drunk'/ard
drunk'en
dry'—/clean'
dry clean'/ing, *n.*
dry goods
dry'ly
dry'/ness
du'al (twofold)
du'bi/ous·ly
Du·buque', Iowa
duch'/ess
duck'/pin'
duc'/tile
due bill
du'el (combat)
du·et'
duf'/fel
dug'/out
dull'/ard
dul'ly
du'ly
dumb'/bell'
dumb'/wait'er
dum'my (/mies)
dump'i/ness
dun'/ga/rees', *pl.*
du'plex
du'pli/cate
du'pli/ca'/tion
du·plic'/i·ty (·ties
Du·quesne', Pa.
du'ra/bil'/i·ty
du'ra/ble
du·ra'/tion
du'ress
dur'/ing
dusk'y
dust bowl
dust'er
dust storm

du'te/ous
du'ti/a · ble
du'ti/ful
du'ty (· ties)
dwell'/ing
dwin'/dle
dyed (stained)
dye'/ing (staining)
dy'ing (pert. to death)
dy · nam'ic
dy'na/mite
dy'na · mo (/mos)
dy'nas · ty (/ties)
dys'en/ter'y
dys/pep'/sia
dys'/tro/phy

E

ea'ger/ness
ea'gle
ear'/ache'
ear'/drum'
ear'/li/est
ear'ly
ear'/nest · ly
ear'/ring'
earth'/quake'
earth'y
ease'/ment
eas'i/est
eas'i · ly
Eas'/ter
east'/er · ly
East'/ern · er
eas'y/go'/ing
ebb'/ing
eb'o · ny (/ies)
ec · cen'/tric
ec'cen/tric'/i · ty (· ties)
ec · cle'/si/as'/ti/cal
ech'e/lon
ech'o (/oes)
é · clair'
ec · lec'/tic
e · clipse'
e'co/nom'ic
e'co/nom'/i · cal · ly
e · con'o/mist
e · con'o · my (/mies)
ec'sta · sy (/sies)
ec · stat'ic
ec'u/men'/i · cal
ec · ze'ma
edge'/ways'
edge'/wise

ed'i·ble
e'dict
ed'i/fi/ca'/tion
ed'i/fice
ed'i·fy
Ed'in/burg, Texas
Ed'in/burgh, Scotland
ed'it
e·di'/tion
ed'i/tor
ed'i/to'/ri·al
ed'i/tor in chief'
ed'u/cate
ed'u/ca'/tion
ed'u/ca'/tor
ef·face'
ef·fect', *n.* (result)
ef·fect', *v.* (bring about)
ef·fec'/tive/ness
ef·fec'/tu/al·ly
ef·fem'i/nate
ef'fer/ves'/cence
ef'fi/ca'/cious
ef'fi/ca·cy (/cies)
ef·fi'/cien·cy (/cies)
ef·fi'/cient
ef'fi·gy (/gies)
ef'fort
ef·fron'/ter·y (/ies)
ef·fu'/sive
egg'/nog'
egg'/plant'
e'go (·gos)
e'go/cen'/tric
e'go/ist
e'go/tist
e'go/tis'/ti/cal
e·gre'/gious
eight'/eenth'
eight'i/eth
ei'ther
e·ject'
e·jec'/tion
eked
e·lab'o/rate
e·lab'o/ra'/tion
e·lapse'
e·las'/tic
e·las'/tic'/i·ty
e·lat'ed
e·la'/tion
el'bow
eld'er (older)
el'der (a tree)
eld'/est
e·lect'
e·lec'/tion
e·lec'/tion/eer'
e·lec'/tive
e·lec'/tor
e·lec'/tor·al
e·lec'/tric
e·lec'/tri/cal

e·lec'/tri'/cian
e·lec'/tric'/i·ty
e·lec'/tri/fied
e·lec'/tri·fy
e·lec'/tro/car'/di·o-/gram'
e·lec'/tro/cute
e·lec'/trode
e·lec'/trol'y/sis
e·lec'/tro/mag'/net
e·lec'/tron
e·lec'/tron'/ics
el'·ee/mos'y/nar'y
el'e/gance
el'e·gy (/gies)
el'e/ment
el·e/men'/tal
el'e/men'/ta·ry
el'e/phant
el'e/vate
el'e/vat'ed
el'e/va'/tion
el'e/va'/tor
e·lic'it (to draw out)
el'i/gi/bil'/i·ty (·ties)
el'i/gi/ble
e·lim'i/nate
e·lim'i/na'/tion
e·lite'
el·lipse'
el·lip'/sis (/ses)
el·lip'/tic
el·lip'/ti/cal
el'o/cu'/tion
e·lon'/gate
el'o/quence
else'/where
e·lu'/ci/date
e·lude' (escape)
e·lu'/sive
e·ma'/ci/at·ed
e·ma'/ci·a'/tion
em'a/nate
e·man'/ci/pate
e·man'/ci/pa'/tion
em·balm'
em·bank'/ment
em·bar'go (/goes)
em·bark'
em'bar/ka'/tion
em·bar'/rass
em·bar'/rass/ment
em'bas·sy (/sies)
em·bez'/zled
em'blem
em·bod'i/ment
em·bod'y
em'bo/lism
em·boss'
em·brace'
em·broi'/der·y (/ies)
em·broil'
em'bry·o (·os)
em'bry/on'ic

em'cee'
em'er/ald
e·merge'
e·mer'/gen·cy (/cies)
e·mer'i/tus (·ti)
em'er·y
em'i/grant
em'i/gra'/tion
em'i/nence (high rank)
em'is/sar'y (/ies)
e·mis'/sion
e·mit'
e·mit'/ted
e·mol'/li/ent (softening)
e·mol'u/ment (salary)
e·mo'/tion
e·mo'/tion/al/ism
em'pa/thy
em'per·or
em'pha/sis (/ses)
em'pha/size
em·phat'ic
em'pire
em·pir'/i·cal
em·ploy'
em·ploy'ee
em·ploy'er
em·ploy'/ment
em·po'/ri·um (/ums)
em·pow'er
emp'/tied
emp'/ti/ness
emp'ty
em'u/late
em'u/la'/tion
e·mul'/si·fy
e·mul'/sion
en·a'ble
en·act'
en·am'el
en·am'/eled
en·ceph'a/li'/tis
en·chant'
en·chant'/ment
en·cir'/cle
en·close'
en·clo'/sure
en·com'/pass
en'core
en·coun'/ter
en·cour'/age
en·croach'
en·cum'/ber
en·cum'/brance
en·cyc'/li/cal
en·cy'/clo/pe'/di·a
en·dan'/ger
en·dear'
en·deav'or
en·dem'ic
end'/less
en'do/crine
en·dorse'

en·dow′
en·dur′/a·ble
en·dur′/ance
en·dure′
end′/ways′
en′e·ma
en′e·my (/mies)
en′er/get′ic
en′er/get′/i·cal·ly
en′er·gy (/gies)
en′er/vate
en·fold′
en·force′
en·force′/a·ble
en·fran′/chise
en·gage′
en·gag′/ing·ly
en·gen′/der
en′gine
en′gi/neer′
En′ glish
En′ glish/man (/men)
en·graft′
en·grain′
en·grave′
en·grav′er
en·gross′
en·gulf′
en·hance′
e·nig′ma
e′nig/mat′ic
en·join′
en·joy′
en·joy′/a·ble
en·large′/ment
en·light′en
en·list′
en·list′/ment
en·liv′en
en masse′
en′mi·ty (/ties)
en′nui′
e·nor′/mi·ty (/ties)
e·nor′/mous
e·nough′
en·rage′
en·rap′/ture
en·rich′
en·roll′
en·rolled′
en·roll′/ment
en route′
en·sem′/ble
en′sign
en·slave′
en·snare′
en·sue′
en·su′/ing
en·tail′
en·tan′/gle
en′ter
en′ter/prise
en′ter/pris′/ing·ly
en′ter/tain′

en′ter/tain′/ment
en·thrall′
en·throne′
en·thu′/si/asm
en·thu′/si/as′/tic
en·thu′/si/as′/ti-
/cal·ly
en·tice′
en·tic′/ing·ly
en·tire′
en·tire′ty
en·ti′/tle
en′ti·ty (/ties)
en′to/mol′o·gy
en·train′
en′trance, *n.* (door)
en·trance′, *v.* (carry away with rapture)
en′trant
en·treat′y (/ies)
en′trée
en′tre/pre/neur′
en·trust′
en′try (·tries)
e·nu′/mer/ate
e·nu′/mer·a′/tion
e·nun′/ci/ate
e·nun′/ci·a′/tion
en·vel′op, *v.*
en′ve/lope, *n.*
en·vel′/oped
en·vel′/op/ing
en′vi/a·ble
en′vied
en′vi/ous
en·vi′/ron/ment
en·vis′/age
en′voy
en′vy
en′zyme
e·phem′/er·al
ep′ic
ep′i/dem′ic
ep′i/der′/mis
ep′i/gram
ep′i/graph
ep′i/lep′sy
ep′i/lep′/tic
ep′i/logue
e·pis′/co/pal
E·pis′/co/pa′/lian
ep′i/sode
e·pis′/tle
ep′i/taph
ep′i/thet
e·pit′o·me
e·pit′o/mize
ep′och
eq′ua/ble
eq′ua/bly
e′qual
e′qualed
e·qual′/i·ty (·ties)

e'qual/ize
e'qual·i/za'/tion
e'qual·ly
e'qua/nim'/i·ty
e·quate'
e·qua'/tion
e·qua'/tor
e'qua/to'/ri·al
e'qui/dis'/tant
e'qui/lat'/er·al
e'qui/lib'/ri·um
e·quip'/ment
e·quipped'
e·quip'/ping
eq'ui/ta/ble
eq'ui·ty (/ties)
e·quiv'a/lent
e·quiv'o/cal
e'ra
e·ra'/di/ate
e·rad'i/ca/ble
e·rad'i/cate
e·ras'/a·ble
e·rase'
e·ras'er
e·ra'/sure
e·rect'
e·rec'/tion
e·rect'ly
E'rie, Pa.
er'mine
e·rode'
e·ro'/sion
er'rand
er'rant
er·rat'ic
er·ra'/tum (·ta)
err'/ing·ly
er·ro'/ne/ous
er'ror
er'u/dite
e·rupt'
e·rup'/tion
er'y/sip'e/las
es'ca/la'/tor
es'ca/pade'
es·cape'
es·cape'/ment
es'cort, *n.*
es·cort', *v.*
es'crow'
e·soph'a/gus (·gi)
es'o/ter'ic
es·pe'/cial
es'pi·o/nage
es'pla/nade'
es'prit' de corps'
es' quire
es'say, *n.*
es·say', *v.*
es'sence
es·sen'/tial
es·tab'/lish
es·tate'

es·teem′
es·thet′·ic
es′ti/mate
es′ti/ma′/tion
es·top′
es·topped′
es·top′/pel
es·trange′/ment
et cet′/er·a
etch′/ing
e·ter′/nal
e·ter′/ni·ty
e′ther
e·the′/re·al
eth′/i·cal
eth′/ics
E′thi·o′/pi·an
eth′yl
eth′/yl/ene
et′i/quette
é′tude
et′y/mol′o/gist
et′y/mol′o·gy
eu′ca/lyp′/tus
eu·gen′/ics
eu′lo/gize
eu′lo·gy (/gies)
eu′phe/mism
eu·pho′/ni/ous
eu′pho·ny (/nies)
eu·re′ka
Eu′ro/pe′an
eu·then′/ics
e·vac′u/ate
e·vac′u/a′tion
e·vac′u·ee′
e·vade′
e·val′u/ate
e·val′u/a′tion
e′van/gel′/i·cal
e·van′/ge/lism
e·van′/ge/lis′/tic
e·vap′o/rate
e·vap′o/ra′/tion
e·va′/sive
eve′/ning
e′ven·ly
e′ven/ness
e·vent′/ful
e·ven′/tu·al
e·ven′/tu/al′/i·ty
(·ties)
ev′er
ev′er/green′
ev′er/last′/ing
ev′er/more′
ev′er·y
ev′er·y/bod′y, *sing.*
ev′er·y/day′, *adj.*
ev′er·y/one′, *sing.*
ev′er·y/thing′
ev′er·y/where′
e·vict′
e·vic′/tion

ev'i/dence
e'vil·ly
e'vil—/mind'ed
e·vince'
ev'o/ca/ble
e·voc'a/tive
e·voke'
ev'o/lu'/tion
ev'o·lu'/tion/ar'y
e·volve'
e·vul'/sion
ex·ac'/er/bate
ex·ac'/er/ba'/tion
ex·act'
ex·ag'/ger/ate
ex·ag'/ger·a'/tion
ex·alt'
ex'al/ta'/tion
ex·alt'ed
ex·am'i/na'/tion
ex·am'/ine
ex·am'/ple
ex·as'/per/ate
ex·as'/per·a'/tion
ex'ca/vate
ex'ca/va'/tion
ex·ceed'
ex·cel'
ex·celled'
ex'cel/lence
ex'cel/len·cy (/cies)
ex·cel'/ling
ex·cel'/si·or
ex·cept'
ex·cep'/tion·al
ex'cerpt, *n.*
ex·cerpt', *v.*
ex·cess'
ex·ces'/sive
ex·change'
ex·change'/a·ble
ex·cis'/a·ble
ex'cise
ex·ci'/sion
ex·cit'a/bil'/i·ty
ex·cit'/a·ble
ex'ci/ta'/tion
ex·cite'
ex·claim'
ex'cla/ma'/tion
ex·clam'a/to'ry
ex·clud'/a·ble
ex·clude'
ex·clu'/sive
ex'com/mu'/ni/cate
ex'com/mu'/ni/ca'/tion
ex·cru'/ci/ate
ex·cru'/ci/at'/ing
ex·cur'/sion
ex·cus'/a·ble
ex·cuse'
ex·cus'/ing
ex'e/cute
ex'e/cu'/tion

ex·ec'u/tive
ex·ec'u/tor
ex·ec'u/to'ry
ex·ec'u/trix
(/tri/ces), *fem.*
ex·em'/pla·ry
ex·em'/pli·fy
ex·empt'
ex·emp'/tion
ex'er/cise
ex·ert'
ex·er'/tion
ex'ha/la'/tion
ex·hale'
ex·haust'
ex·haust'ed
ex·haus'/tion
ex·hib'it
ex'hi/bi'/tion
ex'hi/bi'/tion/ism
ex·hib'i/tor
ex·hil'a/rate
ex·hil'a/ra'/tion
ex·hort'
ex'hor/ta'/tion
ex·hume'
ex'i/gen·cy (/cies)
ex'ile
ex·ist'
ex·ist'/ence
ex'it
ex'o/dus
ex of·fi'/ci·o
ex·on'/er/ate
ex'o/ra/ble
ex·or'/bi/tant
ex'or/cise
ex'or/cism
ex·ot'ic
ex·pand'
ex·panse'
ex·pan'/sion
ex·pa'/tri/ate
ex·pa'/tri·a'/tion
ex·pect'
ex·pec'/tan·cy (/cies)
ex·pec'/tant
ex'pec/ta'/tion
ex·pec'/to/rate
ex·pe'/di/en·cy
(/cies)
ex·pe'/di/ent
ex'pe/dite
ex'pe/di'/tion
ex'pe/di'/tious
ex·pel'
ex·pelled'
ex·pel'/ling
ex·pend'
ex·pen'/di/ture
ex·pense'
ex·pen'/sive
ex·pe'/ri/ence
ex·per'i/ment

ex·per'i/men'/tal
ex·per'i/men/ta'/tion
ex'pert, *n., adj.*
ex'pert·ly
ex'pi/a·ble
ex'pi/ate
ex'pi·a'/tion
ex'pi/ra'/tion
ex·pire'
ex·plain'
ex'pla/na'/tion
ex·plan'a/to'ry
ex'ple/tive
ex·pli'/ca/ble
ex·plic'it
ex·plode'
ex'ploit, *n.*
ex·ploit', *v.*
ex'ploi/ta'/tion
ex'plo/ra'/tion
ex·plor'a/to'ry
ex·plore'
ex·plor'er
ex·plor'/ing
ex·plo'/sion
ex·po'/nent
ex'port, *n.*
ex·port', *v.*
ex'·por/ta'/tion
ex·port'er
ex·pose', *v.*
ex'po·sé', *n.*
ex'po/si'/tion
ex·pos'i/to'ry
ex post fac'to
ex·po'/sure
ex·pound'
ex·press'
ex·pres'/sive
ex·press'ly
ex·press'/man (/men)
ex·pro'/pri/ate
ex·pro'/pri·a'/tion
ex·pul'/sion
ex·qui'/site
ex'tant
ex·tem'/po/ra'/ne/ous
ex·tem'/po/rar'y
ex·tend'
ex·ten'/sion
ex·ten'/sive·ly
ex·tent'
ex·ten'u/ate
ex·ten'u/at'/ing
ex·te'/ri·or
ex·ter'/mi/nate
ex·ter'/mi/na'/tion
ex·ter'/mi/na'/tor
ex·ter'/nal
ex·ter'/nal/ism
ex·tinct'
ex·tinc'/tion
ex·tin'/guish
ex'tir/pate

ex·tol′
ex·tolled′
ex·tol′/ling
ex·tort′
ex·tor′/tion
ex′tra
ex′tract, *n.*
ex·tract′, *v.*
ex·trac′/tion
ex′tra/cur/ric′u/lar
ex′tra/dite
ex′tra/di′/tion
ex′tra/mu′/ral
ex·tra′/ne/ous
ex·traor′/di/nar′i·ly
ex·traor′/di/nar′y
ex·trav′a/gance
ex·trav′a/gan′za
ex·treme′
ex·trem′/i·ty (·ties)
ex′tri/cate
ex·trin′/sic
ex′tro/vert
ex·u′/ber/ance
ex·ude′
ex·ult′
ex′ul/ta′/tion
eye′/ball′
eye′/brow′
eye′/glass′
eye′/lash′
eye′/let
eye′/lid′
eye—/o′pen·er
eye′/sight′
eye′/sore′
eye′/strain′
eye′/tooth′ (/teeth′)
eye′/wash′
eye′/wink′er
eye′/wit′/ness

F

fa′ble
fab′/ric
fab′/ri/ca′/tion
fab′u/lous
fa·cade′
fac′et
fa·ce′/tious
fa′cial
fac′/ile
fa·cil′i/tate
fa·cil′/i·ty (·ties)
fac′/ing

fac/sim'i · le
fac'/tion
fac'/tious
fac'/tor
fac'/to · ry (/ries)
fac'/tu · al
fac'/ul · ty (/ties)
Fahr'/en/heit
faille
fail'/ure
faint'/heart'ed
faint'/ness
fair'ly
fair'—/mind'ed
fair'/ness
fair'y (/ies)
fair'y/land'
faith'/ful
fal/la'/cious
fal'/la · cy (/cies)
fall'en
fal'/li/ble
fall'/out, *n.*
false'/hood
false'ly
fal'/si/fied
fal'/si · fy
fal'/ter
fa · mil'/iar
fa · mil'i/ar'/i · ty
(· ties)
fa · mil'/iar/ize
fa · mil'/iar · ly
fam'i · ly (/lies)
fam'/ished
fa'mous
fa · nat'ic
fa · nat'/i · cal
fa · nat'i/cism
fan'/ci · er
fan'/ci/ful
fan'cy (/cies)
fan'/fare
fanned
fan'/ning
fan/ta'/sia
fan/tas'/tic
fan'/ta · sy (/sies)
far'/a · way'
farce
far'/ci/cal
fare'/well'
far'/fetched'
far'—/flung'
farm'er
farm'/ing
far'—/off', *adj.*
far'—/reach'ing
far'/see'/ing
far'/sight'ed
far'/ther
far'/thest
fas'/ci/nate
fas'/ci/na'/tion

fas'/cist
fash'/ion
fash'/ion · a/bly
fas'/ten
fas/tid'i/ous
fa'tal
fa'tal/ist
fa'tal/is'/tic
fa · tal'/i · ty (· ties)
fa'tal · ly
fat'ed
fate'/ful · ly
fa'ther
fa'ther/hood
fa'ther—/in—/law'
(fa'thers— . . .)
fath'om
fa · tigue'
fat'/ness
fat'/ten
fat'ty
fau'/cet
fault'/find'/ing
fault'i/ness
fault'/less
fault'y
faux pas', *sing. & pl.*
fa'vor/a · ble
fa'vored
fa'vor/ite
fa'vor/it/ism
faze (disturb)

fear'/ful
fea'/si/bil'/i · ty (· ties)
fea'/si/ble
feath'er
feath'/ered
feath'/er · y
fea'/ture
Feb'/ru/ar'y
fed'/er · al
(cap. when pert. to
U. S. Govt.)
fed'/er/al/ist
fed'/er/at · ed
fed'/er · a'/tion
fee'/ble
fee'/ble/mind · ed
feed'/back, *n.*
feel'/ing · ly
feign
feigned
feint
fe · lic'i/tate
fe · lic'i/tous
fe'line
fel'/low/ship
fel'on
fel'o · ny (/nies)
fe'male
fem'i/nine
fem'i/nin'/i · ty (· ties)
fe'mur
(· murs; fem'o · ra)

fend'er
fe·ra'/cious
fe·rac'/i·ty
fer'/ment, *n.*
fer/ment', *v.*
fer'/men/ta'/tion
fe·ro'/cious
fe·roc'/i·ty (·ties)
fer'/ret
fer'ry (/ries)
fer'/tile
fer/til'/i·ty
fer'/ti/lize
fer'/ti/liz'er
fer'/vent
fer'/vid
fer'/vor
fes'/ter
fes'/ti/val
fes'/tive
fes/tiv'/i·ty (·ties)
fes/toon'
fetch'/ing·ly
fete
fet'ed
fe'tish
feu'/dal/ism
fe'ver
fe'ver/ish/ness
fi'an·cé', *masc.*
fi'an/cée', *fem.*
fi·as'co (/coes)
fi'at
fi'ber
Fi'ber/glas'
fi'brous
fib'u·la (/lae; /las)
fick'le
fic'/tion
fic/ti'/tious
fid'/dle
fi·del'/i·ty (·ties)
fi·du'/ci/ar'y (/ies)
field'er
fiend'/ish
fierce
fi'er·y
fies'ta
fif'/teenth'
fif'/ti/eth
fif'ty
fight'er
fig'/ment
fig'/ur·a/tive·ly
fig'/ure
fig'/ure/head'
fig'u/rine'
fil'a/ment
fi'let'
fi'let' de sole'
fi'let' mi'·gnon'
fil'i·al
fil'i/bus'/ter
fil'i/gree

fil'/ing
Fil'i/pi'no (/nos)
fill'er
fil'/let
film'/strip'
filmed
fil'/ter
filth'y
fil/tra'/tion
fi'nal
fi·na'le
fi'nal/ist
fi·nal'/i·ty (·ties)
fi·nance'
fi·nan'/cial·ly
fi'·nan/cier'
find'/ing
fine'ly
fin'/er·y (/ies)
fi·nesse'
fin'/ger
fin'/ger/print'
fi'nis
fin'/ish
fin'/ished
fi'nite
fire'/arms'
fire'/place'
fire'/plug'
fire'/proof'
fir'/ing
fir'/ma/ment
firm'ly
first'—/class', *adj.*
first'/hand'
fis'/cal
fish'/er/man (/men)
fish'/er·y (/ies)
fish'y
fis'/sion
fis'/sure
fit'/ful·ly
fit'/ness
fit'/ted
fix'/ate
fix·a'/tion
fix'/ture
fiz'/zle
flab'by
flag'/ging
fla'/gran·cy (/cies)
flag'/ship'
flag'/staff'
flair (aptitude)
flak'y
flam/boy'/ant
fla/min'go (/gos)
flam'/ma/ble
(inflammable)
flange
flank
flan'/nel
flap'/ping
flare'—up', *n.*

flash'i·ly
flash'/light'
flat'—/foot'ed
flat'/i'ron
flat'/ten
flat'/ter·y
flaunt
fla'/vor
flaw'/less
fledg'/ling
flee'/ing
fleeced
fleet'/ing
flesh'i/ness
fleur'—/de—/lis'
(fleurs'— . . .)
flew
flex'i/bil'/i·ty
flex'/i·ble
flick'er
fli'er
flight'i/ness
flim'/si/ness
flim'sy
flip'/pan·cy
flip'/pant
flir/ta'/tion
flit'/ted
float'/ing
flood'/gate'
flood'/light'
floor'/ing
flo'/ral
flo/res'/cent
(blossoming)
flor'id
flor'in
flo'/rist
flo/ta'/tion
floun'/der
flour'/ish
flour'y
flout
flow'er
flow'/er·y
flown
fluc'/tu/ate
fluc'/tu·a'/tion
flue
flu'/en·cy
flu'/ent
fluff'y
flu'id
flu'o/res'/cent (light)
flu'o/ri/date
flu'o/ro/scope
flur'ry (/ries)
flushed
flus'/ter
flut'/ist
flut'/ter
fly'/leaf' (/leaves')
fly'/wheel
foam'y

ɔ'cal
ɔ'cus (· cus · es; · ci)
ɔd'/der
ɔg'gy
ɔld'er
ɔ'li/age
ɔ'li · o (· os)
ɔlk'/lore'
ɔl'/low
ɔl'low—up', *n.*
ɔl'ly
ɔ · ment' (rouse)
ɔn'/dle
ɔnd'/ness
ɔod'/stuff'
ɔol'/har'dy
ɔol'/ish
ɔol'/proof'
ɔot'/ball'
ɔot/can'/dle
ɔot'/hold'
ɔot'/note'
ɔot'/wear
ɔr'/age
ɔr/bade'
ɔr/bear'/ance
ɔr/bid'
ɔr/bid'/den
ɔr/bore'
ɔrced
ɔrce'/ful · ly
ɔr'/ceps

for'/ci/bly
forc'/ing
fore'/arm', *n.*
fore/arm', *v.*
fore/bode'
fore/bod'/ing
fore/cast', *v.*
fore'/cast', *n.*
fore/cast'er
fore/close'
fore/clo'/sure
fore'/fa'/ther
fore'/fin'/ger
fore'/front'
fore/go'/ing
fore/gone'
fore'/hand'ed
fore'/head
for'/eign
for'/eign · er
fore'/man (/men)
fore'/most
fore'/noon'
fo · ren'/sic
fore/run'/ner
fore/see'
fore/shad'ow
fore'/sight'/ed/ness
for'/est
fore/stall'
for'/est · er
for'/est · ry

fore/tell′
fore′/thought′
for/ev′·er
for/ev′/er/more′
fore/warn′
fore′/word′ (preface)
for′/feit
for′/fei/ture
for/gave′
forg′er
forg′/er·y (/ies)
for/get′
for/get′/ful/ness
for/giv′/a·ble
for/give′
for/give′/ness
for/got′/ten
forked
for/lorn′
for′/mal
form/al′/de/hyde
for/mal′/i·ty (·ties)
for′/mal/ize
for′/mat
for/ma′/tion
for′/ma/tive
form′er, *n.*
for′/mer, *adj.*
for′/mi/da/ble
for′/mu·la (/las; /lae)
for′/mu/late
for/sake′
for/syth′i·a
forth′/com′/ing
forth′/right′
forth′/with′
for′/ti/eth
for′/ti/fi/ca′/tion
for′/ti/fied
for′/ti·fy
for/tis′/si·mo
for′/ti/tude
for′/tress
for/tu′i/tous
for′/tu/nate·ly
for′/tune
for′ty (/ties)
fo′rum (·rums; ·ra)
for′/ward
(toward the front)
fos′/sil
fos′/ter
fought
foul (bad)
foun/da′/tion
found′er, *n.*
foun′/der, *v.*
found′/ling
found′ry (/ries)
foun′/tain
four′/some
four′/teenth′
fowl (poultry)
fox′/hole′

x'i/ness
x'y
y'er
a'/cas
ac'/tion
ac'/tious
ac'/ture
ag'/ile
ag'/ment
ag'/men/tar'y
a'/grant
ail'ty (/ties)
ame'—up', *n.*
ame'/work'
anc (coin)
an'/chise
rank'/fort, Ky.
ank'/furt · er
ank'ly
an'/tic
ap'pé'
a/ter'/nal · ly
a/ter'/ni · ty (/ties)
at'/er/nize
aud'u/lent
ee'/dom
ee lance, *n.*
ee'—/lance', *adj.*, *v.*
ee'ly
ree on board
(f.o.b.; F.O.B.)
eeze

freight'er
fren'zy (/zies)
fre'/quen · cy (/cies)
fre'/quent, *adj.*
fre/quent', *v.*
fres'co (/coes)
fresh'/man (/men)
fresh'/ness
fret'/ful · ly
Freud'i · an
fric'/as/see'
fric'/tion
Fri'/day
friend'/li/ness
friend'/ship
frieze
fright
fright'/ened
frig'id
fri/gid'/i · ty
frill'y
fringe
frit'/ter
fri/vol'/i · ty (· ties)
friv'o/lous
frog'/man (/men)
frol'/ic/some
front'/age
fron'/tal
fron/tier'
fron'/tis/piece
frost'i/ness

frost'y
froth'y
frowned
froze
fro'/zen
fru'/gal
fruit'/ful
fru·i'/tion
frus'/trate
frus/tra'/tion
fuch'/sia
fu'el
fu'gi/tive
fugue
ful/fill'
ful/fill'/ment
full'/back'
full'—/fash'ioned
ful'ly
ful'/mi/nate
ful'/some
fum'/ble
fumed
fu'mi/gate
func'/tion·al
fun/da/men'/tal·ly
fun/da/men'/tal/ist
fu'ner·al
fun'/gus (·gi)
fun'/nel
fun'ny
fur'/bish
fu'ri/ous
fur'/lough
fur'/nace
fur'/nish
fur'/ni/ture
fu'ror
fur'/ri·er
fur'/row
fur'ry
fur'/ther
fur'/ther/more'
fur'/thest
fur'/tive·ly
fu'ry (·ries)
fuse
fu'se/lage
fu'si/ble
fu'sion
fuss'i/ness
fuss'y
fu'tile
fu·til'/i·ty (·ties)
fu'ture
fu·tu'/ri·ty (/ties)
fuzz'y

G

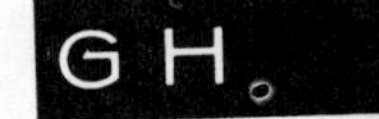

ab'/ar/dine'
a'ble
ad'/get
ai'e·ty (/ties)
ain'/ful
ain'/li/ness
ait
a'la
al'/ax·y
al'/lant·ly
al'/lant·ry (/ries)
al'/le·on (ship)
al'/ler·y (/ies)
gal'/ley (leys)
gall'/ing
gal'/lon
gal'/lop
gal'/lop/ing
gal'/loped
gal'/lows
gall'/stone'
ga·lore'
gal'/va/ni/za'/tion
gal'/va/nize
gam'/ble
gam'/bler
gam'/bling
game'ly
gam'ut
gan'/der
gan'/gling
gang'/plank'
gan'/grene
gang'/ster
gang'/way'
gap'/ping
ga·rage'
gar'/bage
gar'/bled
gar'/den
gar'/den·er
gar/de'/ni·a
gar'/gle
gar'/goyle
gar'/ish
gar'/land
gar'/lic
gar'/ment
gar'/ner
gar'/net
gar'/nish
gar'/nish/ment
gar'/ret
gar'/ri/son

gar/ru'/li·ty
gar'/ru/lous
gar'/ter
gas'/eous
gas'/ket
gas'/light'
gas mask
gas·o/line'
gas sta'/tion
gas'/tric
gas'/tro/nom'ic
gas/tron'o·my
gate'/way'
gath'er
gath'/er/ing
gauche
gaud'y
gauge
gaunt'/ness
gauze
gav'el
gawk'y
gay'/ness
ga·zelle'
ga·zette'
gaz'/et/teer'
gear'/shift'
Gei'/ger count'er
gei'/sha
gel'a/tin
ge·lat'i/nate
ge·lat'i/nous
gen/darme'
gen'/der
gen'e/al'o·gy (/gies)
gen'/er·al
gen'/er·a/lis'/si·mo (/mos)
gen'/er/al'/i·ty (·ties)
gen'/er/al·i/za'/tion
gen'/er/al/ize
gen'/er/al·ly
gen'/er/al/ship'
gen'/er/ate
gen'/er·a'/tion
gen'/er·a'/tive
gen'/er·a'/tor
ge·ner'ic
gen'/er/os'/i·ty (·ties)
gen'/er/ous
ge·net'/ics
gen'e/sis
ge'nial
ge'ni/al'/i·ty
ge'nial·ly
ge'nius
gen/teel'
gen'/tile
gen/til'/i·ty (·ties)
gen'/tle
gen'/tle/man (/men)
gen'/tle/ness

nt'ly
n'u/ine
'nus (gen'/er·a)
·og'/ra/pher
'o/graph'ic
'o/graph'/i·cal
·og'/ra/phy
(/phies)
'o/log'/i·cal
·ol'o/gist
·ol'o·gy (/gies)
'o/met'/ric
'o/met'/ri/cal
·om'e/try (/tries)
·o/phys'/i·cal
or'/gi·an
·ra'/ni·um
r'i/at'/rics
r'/man (/mans)
r/mane'
r'/mi/cide
r'/mi/nate
r'/mi/na'/tion
r'/und
s'/tate
s/ta'/tion
s/tic'u/late
s/tic'u/la'/tion
s'/ture
t'/a·way', *n.*
y'/ser
ast'/li/ness

ghast'ly
ghost'/like'
ghost'ly
gi'ant
gibe
Gi·bral'/tar
gid'/di·ly
gid'/di/ness
gid'dy
gift'ed
gi·gan'/tic
gild'ed
gilt'—/edged'
gim'/mick
gin'/ger
gin'/ger/bread'
gin'/ger·ly
ging'/ham
gi·raffe'
gird'er
gir'/dle
girl'/hood
girl'/ish
give'—/and—/take', *n.*
give'/a·way, *n.*
giv'en
giv'er
gla'/cial
gla'/cier
glad'/den
gla'/di·o'/lus
glad'ly

glad'/ness
glam'/or/ous
glam'/our
glanc'/ing
glan'/du/lar
glar'/ing · ly
glass'/ful
glass'i/ness
glass'/ware'
glass'y
glau/co'ma
glazed
glean'/ing
glee'/ful · ly
glib'ly
glid'er
glid'/ing
glim'/mer
glim'/mer/ing
glimps'/ing
glis'/ten
glit'/ter
glit'/ter · y
glob'al
glob'u/lar
globe'—/trot'ter
gloom'i · ly
gloom'i/ness
gloom'y
glo'/ri/fi/ca'/tion
glo'/ri · fy
glo'/ri/ous
glo'ry (/ries)
glos'/sa · ry (/ries)
gloss'i/ness
gloss'y
glow'/ing · ly
glu'/cose
glu'/ing
glum'ly
glum'/ness
glu'/ti/nous (gluey)
glut'/ton
glut'/ton/ous (voraciou
glyc'/er · in
gnarled
gnash
gnaw'/ing
go'—/a · head', *n., adj.*
gob'/ble
gob'/ble/dy/gook'
go'—/be · tween', *n.*
gob'/let
go/cart'
god'/child'
(/chil'/dren)
god'/dess
god'/fa'/ther
god'/head
god'/less
god'/like'
god'ly
god'/moth'er
god'/par'/ent

od'/send′
od'/speed′
o′—/get′ter
og'/gle
o′ing
oi′/ter
old'/brick′
old dig'/ger
old'en
old'en rule
old'/fish′, *sing. & pl.*
olf'er
on′/or/rhe'a
ood—/bye'
ood′/heart'ed
ood'ly
ood′—/na'tured
ood'/ness
ood′—/tem'pered
ood/will
ood'y (/ies)
oose'/ber′ry (/ries)
o'pher
orged
or'/geous
o·ril'la
or'y
os'/pel
os'/sip/ing
Goth'ic
ouge
ourd

gour'/mand
gour'/met
gov'/ern
gov'/ern/a·ble
gov'/er/ness
gov'/ern/men'/tal
gov'/er/nor
gov'/er/nor—gen'/er·al
gov'/er/nor/ship′
grabbed
grace'/ful/ness
gra'/cious
gra/da'/tion
grad'u·al
grad'u/ate
grad′u/a'tion
graft'er
gra'/ham
grain'y
gram
gram'/mar
gram/mar'i·an
gram/mat'/i·cal
gran'a·ry (/ries)
grand'/child′
(/chil′/dren)
grand'/daugh'/ter
gran'/deur
grand'/fa′/ther
gran/dil'o/quent
gran'/di/ose
grand'/moth′er

grand'/son'
grand'/stand'
gran'/ite
gran'/tee'
grant'—/in—/aid'
(grants'— . . .)
grant'or
gran'u/lar
gran'u/lat'ed
gran'u/la'/tion
gran'/ule
grape'/fruit'
graph'ic
graph'/i·cal·ly
graph'/ite
grap'/ple
grasp'/ing
grass'/hop'/per
grass'y
grate'/ful
grat'i/fi/ca'/tion
grat'i/fied
grat'i/fy'/ing
grat'/ing
gra'/tis
grat'i/tude
gra/tu'i/tous
gra/tu'/i·ty (·ties)
grav'el
grave'ly
grav'en
grave'/stone'
grave'/yard'
grav'i/tate
grav'i/ta'/tion
grav'/i·ty (·ties)
gra'vy (/vies)
gray'/ish
gray'/ness
graz'/ing
greas'i/ness
greas'y
great'/heart'ed
greed'i·ly
greed'y
green'/back'
green'/er·y (/ies)
green'—/eyed'
green'/horn'
green'/house'
green'/ish
greet'/ing
gre/gar'i/ous
Gre/go'/ri·an
gre/nade'
gren'a/dier'
grey'/hound'
grid
grid'/dle
grid'/i'ron
grief'—/strick'en
griev'/ance
griev'/ous
gri'/mace

grime
grim'i/ness
grim'ly
grim'/ness
grim'y
grind'/stone'
grin'/ning
grip (grasp)
gripe (complain)
grippe (sickness)
grip'/ping
gris'/tle
gris'ly
grits
grit'ty
griz'/zly
groaned
gro'/cer · y (/ies)
grog'gy
groin
groomed
groove
grop'/ing · ly
gros'/grain'
gross'ly
gro/tesque'
grouch'i/ness
ground crew
ground floor
ground'/hog
ground'/less
ground'/work'
group'/ing
grouse
grow'er
growled
grown'—up', *adj., n.*
grub'/bing
grudge
grudg'/ing · ly
gru'/el/ing
grue'/some
gruff'ly
grum'/bled
grum'/bling
guar'/an/tee'
guar'/an/teed'
guar'/an/tee'/ing
guar'/an/tor
guar'/an · ty (/ties)
guard'/house'
guard'i · an
guard'i/an/ship'
gua'va
gu'ber/na/to'/ri · al
guer/ril'la
guess'/work'
guest
guid'/ance
guid'ed
guild
guile'/ful · ly
guilt'i · ly
guilt'i/ness

guilt'/less
guilt'y
guin'ea
guise
gui/tar'
gulf
gul'/let
gul'/li/bil'/i·ty
gul'/li/ble
gul'ly (/lies)
gulp'/ing·ly
gum'/drop'
gum'my
gump'/tion
gun'/fire'
gun'/met·al
gun'/ner
gun'/pow'/der
gun'/shot'
gup'py (/pies)
gur'/gle
gush'er
gus'/set
gus'to
gust'y
gut'/ter
gut'/tur·al
guz'/zle
gym/na'/si/ast
gym/na'/si·um
gym'/nast
gym/nas'/tics
gyn'e/col'o·gy
gyn'e/col'o/gist
gyp'/sum
Gyp'/sy (/sies)
gy'rate
gy·ra'/tion
gy'ro/scope

H

ha'be·as cor'/pus
ha·bil'i/tate
hab'it
hab'/it/a·ble
ha'bi/tant
hab'i/tat
hab'i/ta'/tion
ha·bit'u·al
hack'/neyed
had'/dock
hag'/gard
hag'/gle
hail'/stone'
hail'/storm'

ıairs'/breadth'
ıair'/cut'
ıair'do' (/dos')
ıair'i/ness
ıalf (halves)
ıalf'/back'
ıalf'—/breed'
ıalf'—dol'lar
ıalf'/heart'/ed·ly
ıalf hour, *n.*
ıalf—/hour, *adj.*
ıalf—/mast
ıalf'/way'
ıalf'—/wit'
ıal'i/but
ıal'i/to'/sis
ıal'/low
Hal'/low/een'
ıal/lu'/ci/na'/tion
ıall'/way'
ıa'lo (·los)
ıal'/ter
ıalt'/ing·ly
ıam'/burg·er
ıam'/mer
ıam'/mock
ıam'/per
ıam'/ster
ıam'/string'
Ham/tramck', Mich.
hand'/bag'
hand'/ball'
hand'/book'
hand'/ful
hand'i/cap
hand'i/craft
hand'i·ly
hand'i/work'
hand'/ker/chief
(/chiefs)
han'/dle
han'/dling
hand'/made'
hand'/out'
hand'/some
hand'/writ/ing
hand'y/man (/men)
han'/gar (shelter)
hang'er
(device for hanging)
hang'/nail'
hang'/over, *n.*
han'/ker/ing
hap'/haz'/ard
hap'/pen/ing
hap'/pi·ly
hap'/pi/ness
hap'py
hap'py—/go—/luck'y
ha·rangue'
ha·rass'
har'/bin/ger
har'/bor
hard'—/boiled'

hard'en
hard'/head'ed
hard'/heart'ed
har'/di/ness
hard'ly
hard'/ness
hard'/ship
hard'/ware'
hard'/wood'
har'dy
hare'/brained'
harm'/less/ness
har/mon'i·ca
har/mo'/ni/ous
har'/mo/nize
har'/mo·ny (/nies)
har'/ness
harp'/ist
har/poon'
har'/ried
Har'/ris/burg, Pa.
har'/row
har'ry
harsh'/ness
har'/vest
has'—/been', *n.*
has'/sle
has'/sock
has'/ten
hast'i·ly
hast'y
hatch'/er·y (/ies)
hatch'et
hate'/ful·ly
ha'tred
haugh'ty
haugh'/ti/ness
hauled
haunt'/ing·ly
Ha·van'a
ha'ven
hav'oc
Ha·wai'/ian
hawk'er
hay fev'er
hay'/field'
hay'/seed'
haz'/ard
haz'/ard/ous
haz'el
ha'zi/ness
haz'/ing
ha'zy
H'—bomb'
head'/ache'
head'/light'
head'/long
head'—on'
head'/quart'/ters,
sing. & pl.
head'/strong
head'/way'
healed
health'/ful

ealth'i·ly
ealth'i/ness
ealth'y
eaped
ear'/ing
ear'/say'
eart'/ache'
eart'/break'/ing
eart'/bro'/ken
eart'/burn'
eart'en
earth'/stone'
eart'i·ly
eart'/less
eart'/rend/ing
eart'/sick'
eart'y
eat'er
ea'/then/ish
eath'er
eav'/en·ly
eav'/en/ward
eav'i·ly
eav'y
eav'y—/du'ty, *adj.*
eav'y/weight'
eck'le
ec'/tic
ec'/to/graph
edge
eed'/less/ness
eel

heif'er
height
height'en
heir
heir'/ess
heir'/loom'
he'li/cop/ter
he'li·um
hel·lo'
hel'/met
help'er
help'/ful/ness
help'/mate'
hel'ter—/skel'ter
hem'i/sphere
hem'i/spher'ic
hem'/lock
hem'/ming
hem'o/glo'/bin
he'mo/phil'i·a
he'mo/phil'i·ac
hem'/or/rhage
hem'/or/rhoid
hem'/stitch'
hence'/forth'
hence'for'/ward
hench'/man (/men)
hep'a/ti'/tis
her'/ald
her/ba'/ceous
herb'/age
Her/cu'/le·an

here/aft′er
here • by′
he • red′i/tar′y
he • red′/i • ty (• ties)
here • in′
her′e • sy (/sies)
her′e/tic
here′/to/fore′
here/with′
her′/it/age
her/met′ic
her′/mit
her′/mit/age
her′/ni • a
he′ro (• roes)
he • ro′ic
her′o/ine
her′o/ism
her/self′
hes′i/tan • cy (/cies)
hes′i/tate
hes′i/ta′/tion
het′/er • o/ge/ne′/i • ty (• ties)
het′/er • o/ge′/ne/ous
hex′a/gon
hex/ag′o/nal
hey′/day′
hi′ber/nate
hi′ber/na′/tion
hic′/cup
hick′o • ry (/ries)
hid′/den
hid′e/ous
hi′er/ar′/chy
hi′er • o/glyph′ • ic
hi′—fi′
high′/ball′
high′/boy′
high′/brow′
high′/hand′ed
high′/land
high′/ness
high′—/pres′sure, *v., adj*
high school
high′—/spir′it • ed
high′—/strung′
high′—/test′
high′/way′
hi′—jack
hi • lar′i/ous
hi • lar′/i • ty
hill′/side′
hill′y
him/self′
hin′/der, *v.*
hin′/drance
hind′/sight′
hinge
hing′/ing
hint′/ing
hiss′/ing
his′/ta/mine
his′/to/gram

his/to′/ri·an
his/tor′ic
his/tor′/i·cal
his′/to·ry (/ries)
his′/tri/on′ic
hit′—/and—/miss′, *adj.*
hit′—/and—/run′, *adj.*
hitch′/hike′
hith′/er·to′
hoard′/ing
hoarse′/ness
hoax
hob′/ble
hob′/nob′
ho′bo (·boes)
hock′ey
ho′cus—/po′cus
hoe′/ing
hog′/gish·ly
hoi pol/loi′
hoist′ed
hold′er
hold′up′
hole′y (having holes)
hol′i/day
ho′li/ness
hol′/low
hol′ly (shrub)
hol′o/caust
hol′/ster
ho′ly (sacred)
hom′/age
home′/less
home′/li/ness
home′ly
home′/made′
home′/mak′/ing
home run
home′/sick′
home′/stead
home′/work′
hom′i/cide
hom′i·ly (/lies)
hom′i·ny
ho′mo/ge/ne′/i·ty
(·ties)
ho′mo/ge′/ne/ous
ho·mog′e/nized
hom′o/nym
ho′mo/sex′u·al
hon′/est
hon′/es·ty
hon′/ey/bee′
hon′/ey/comb′
hon′/ey/moon′
hon′/ey/suck′le
hon′or
hon′/or/a·ble
hon′o/rar′i·um
(·i·a; /ums)
hon′/or/ar′y
hood′ed
hood′/lum
hoo′/doo

hood'/wink
hook'up'
hope'/ful
hope'/less/ness
hop'/per
hop'/ping
ho·ri'/zon
hor'i/zon'/tal
hor'/mone
hor'/net
ho·rol'o·gy
hor'o/scope
hor'/ri/ble
hor'/rid
hor'/ri·fy
hor'/ror
horse'/back'
horse'/pow'er
horse'—/rad'ish
horse sense
horse'/shoe'
hor'/ti/cul'/tur/ist
hor'/ti/cul'/ture
ho'sier·y
hos/pi'/ta/ble
hos'/pi/tal
hos'/pi/tal'/i·ty (·ties)
hos'/pi/tal/ize
hos'/pi/tal·i/za'/tion
hos'/tage
hos'/tel·ry (/ries)
host'/ess
hos'/tile
hos/til'/i·ty (·ties)
hot dog
ho·tel'
hot'/head'ed
hot'/house'
hot'ly
hot rod
hour'ly
house'/break'/ing
house'/bro'ken
house'/coat'
house'/hold
hous'/ing
house'/keep'er
house'/wife' (/wives')
house'/work'
Hous'/ton, Tex.
hov'el
hov'er
how/ev'er
hub'/bub
huck'/ster
hud'/dle
huff'i·ly
huff'y
huge'/ness
hugged
hul'/la/ba/loo'
hu'man
hu·mane'

hu'man/ism
hu'man/is'/tic
hu·man'i/tar'i·an
hu·man'/i·ty (·ties)
hu'man/kind'
hu'man·ly
hum'/ble/ness
hum'/bly
hum'/drum'
hu'mid
hu·mid'/i·ty
hu·mil'i/ate
hu·mil'i/a'tion
hu·mil'/i·ty
hummed
hum'/ming
hu'mor
hu'mor/ist
hu'mor/ous
hun'/dred
hun'/dredth
hun'/dred/weight'
hun'/ger
hun'/gri·ly
hun'/gry
hunt'er
hur'/dle
Hu'ron
hur'/ri/cane
hur'/ried
hur'ry (/ries)
hus'/band
hus'/band·ry
hush'—/hush', *adj.*
hush mon'ey
husk'i·ly
husk'i/ness
husk'/ing
husk'y
hus'/tle
hy'brid
hy'drant
hy'drat·ed
hy·drau'/lic
hy'dro/chlo'/ric
hy'dro/chlo'/ride
hy'dro/e·lec'/tric
hy'dro/gen
hy'dro/plane
hy'dro/stat'ic
hy'dro/ther'a·py
hy'giene
hy'gi/en'ic
hym'/nal
hy·per'/bo·le
hy'per/sen'/si/tive
hy'per/son'ic
hy'per/ten'/sion
hy'phen
hy'phen/ate
hyp/no'/sis (/ses)
hyp/not'ic
hyp'/no/tism
hy'po/chon'/dri·ac

hy·poc'/ri·sy (/sies)
hyp'o/crite
hyp'o/crit'/i·cal
hy'po/der'/mic
hy·poth'e/sis (/ses)
hy'po/thet'/i·cal
hys'/ter/ec'/to·my
hys/te'/ri·a
hys/ter'/i·cal
hys/ter'/ics

I

i·am'/bic
ice bag
ice'/box'
ice cream
i'ci/cle
i'ci/ness
ic'ing
i'cy
i·de'al
i·de'/al/is'/tic
i·de'/al/ize
i·de'/al·ly
i·den'/ti/cal
i·den'/ti/fi/ca'/tion
i·den'/ti/fies
i·den'/ti·fy
i·den'/ti·ty (/ties)
id'e/ol'o·gy (/gies)
id'i/o·cy (·cies)
id'i·om
id'i/o·mat'ic
id'i/o·syn'/cra·sy (/sies)
id'i·ot
id'i/ot'ic
i'dle/ness
i'dly
i'dol
i'dol/ize
i'dyll
ig·nite'
ig·ni'/tion
ig·no'/ble
ig'no/min'i/ous
ig'no/min·y (/ies)
ig'no/ra'/mus
ig'no/rance
ig·nore'
ill'—/ad·vised'
ill'—/bred'
il'le/gal'/i·ty (·ties)
il·le'/gal·ly

il·leg'/i·ble
il'le/git'i/mate
ill'—/fa'vored
ill'—/hu'mored
il·lic'it (unlawful)
il·lit'/er·a·cy (/cies)
il·lit'/er/ate
ill'—/man'nered
ill'/ness
il·log'/i·cal
ill'—/tem'pered
il·lu'/mi/nate
il·lu'/mi/na'/tion
il/lu'/mine
il·lu'/sion
il'lus/trate
il'lus/tra'/tion
il'lus/tra'/tor
il·lus'/tri/ous
im'age
im'ag/er·y
im·ag'i/nar'y
im·ag'i/na'/tion
im·ag'/ine
im'be/cile
im·bed'
im·bibe'
im·bib'er
im·bued'
im'i/ta/ble
im'i/tate
im'i/ta'/tion
im·mac'u/late
im'ma/te'/ri/al·ly
im'ma/ture'
im'ma/tu'/ri·ty (/ties)
im·mea'/sur/a·ble
im·me'/di·a·cy (/cies)
im·me'/di/ate
im'me/mo'/ri·al
im·mense'
im·men'/si·ty (/ties)
im·merge'
im·merse'
im·mer'/sion
im'mi/grant
im'mi/gra'/tion
im'mi/nent (impending)
im·mo'/bile
im'mo/bil'/i·ty (·ties)
im·mo'/bi/li/za'/tion
im·mo'/bi/lize
im·mod'/er/ate
im·mod'/er·a'/tion
im·mod'/est
im·mor'al
im'mo/ral'/i·ty (·ties)
im·mor'/tal
im'mor/tal'/i·ty
im·mor'/tal/ize
im·mov'/a·ble
im·mune'
im·mu'/ni·ty (/ties)

im·mu′/ta/ble
im·pact′ed
im·pair′/ment
im·pal′/pa/ble
im·pan′el
im·part′
im·par′/tial
im′par/ti/al′/i·ty
im·pass′/a·ble
im′/passe
im·pas′/sioned
im·pas′/sive·ly
im·pa′/tience
im·peach′/ment
im·pec′/ca/ble
im′·pe/cu′/ni/ous
im·ped′/ance
im·pede′
im·ped′i/ment
im·pel′
im·pelled′
im·pel′/ling
im·pend′/ing
im·pen′e/tra/ble
im·per′a/tive
im′per/cep′/ti/ble
im·per′/fect
im′per/fec′/tion
im·per′/fo/rat′ed
im·per′/fo/ra′/tion
im·pe′/ri·al
im·pe′/ri/al/ism
im·per′il
im·per′/iled
im·pe′/ri/ous
im·per′/ish/a·ble
im·per′/ma/nent
im·per′/me/a·ble
im·per′/son·al
im·per′/son/ate
im·per′/son·a′/tion
im·per′/ti/nence
im′per/turb′/a·ble
im·per′/vi/ous
im·pet′·u/os′/i·ty
im·pet′u/ous
im′pe/tus
im·pinge′
im·pla′/ca/ble
im·plant′
im·plau′/si/ble
im′ple/ment
im′ple/men/ta′/tion
im′pli/cate
im′pli/ca′/tion
im·plic′/it·ly
im·plied′
im·plore′
im·plor′/ing·ly
im·ply′
im′po/lite′
im·port′, *v.*
im′port, *n.*
im·por′/tance

m'por/ta'/tion
m·port'er
m·pose'
m'po/si'/tion
m·pos'/si/bil'/i·ty
(·ties)
m·pos'/si/ble
m·pos'/tor
m'po/ten·cy
m'po/tent
im·pound'
im·pov'/er/ish
im·prac'/ti/ca/ble
im·prac'/ti/cal
im'pre/cate
im'pre/ca'/tion
im·preg'/na/ble
im·preg'/nate
im'pre/sa'/ri·o (·os)
im·press', *v.*
im'press, *n.*
im·pres'/sion
im·pres'/sion/a·ble
im·pres'/sive
im·print', *v.*
im'print, *n.*
im·pris'/on/ment
im'prob·a/bil'/i·ty
(·ties)
im·prob'/a·ble
im·promp'tu
im·prop'er
im'pro/pri'e·ty (/ties)
im·prove'/ment
im·prov'i/dent
im'pro/vi/sa'/tion
im'pro/vise
im·pru'/dent
im'pu/dence
im'pu/dent
im·pugn'
im·pugn'/a·ble
im'pulse
im·pul'/sive/ness
im·pu'/ni·ty (/ties)
im·pure'
im·pu'/ri·ty (/ties)
im·put'/a·ble
im'pu/ta'/tion
im·pute'
in'a/bil'/i·ty
in ab·sen'/tia
in'ac/ces'/si/bil'/i·ty
in'ac/ces'/si/ble
in·ac'/cu/ra·cy
(/cies)
in·ac'/cu/rate
in·ac'/tive
in'ac/tiv'/i·ty
in·ad'e/qua·cy (/cies)
in·ad'e/quate·ly
in'ad/mis'/si/ble
in'ad/vert'/ent
in'ad/vis'/a·ble

in·a'lien/a·ble
in·al'/ter/a·ble
in·ane'
in·an'i/mate
in·ap'/pli/ca/ble
in'ap/pre'/cia/bly
in'ap/pre'/ci·a'/tive
in'ap/pre/hen'/si/ble
in'ap/pro'/pri/ate
in'ar/tic'u/late
in'as/much'
in'at/ten'/tive
in·au'/di/ble
in·au'/gu/ral
in·au'/gu/rate
in·au'/gu/ra'/tion
in'aus/pi'/cious
in'born'
in'bred'
in·cal'/cu/la/ble
in'can/des'/cent
in'ca/pa/bil'/i·ty
in·ca'/pa/ble
in'ca/pac'i/tate
in·car'/cer/ate
in·car'/cer·a'/tion
in·car'/nate
in'car/na'/tion
in·cau'/tious
in·cen'/di/ar'y (/ies)
in·cense', *v.*
in'cense, *n.*
in·cen'/tive
in·cep'/tion
in·ces'/sant·ly
in'ci/dence
in'ci/den'/tal
in·cin'/er/ate
in·cin'/er·a'/tor
in·cip'i/ent
in·ci'/sion
in·ci'/sive
in·ci'/sor
in·cite'
in·cite'/ment
in·clem'/ent
in'cli/na'/tion
in·cline', *v.*
in'cline, *n.*
in·clin'/ing
in·clude'
in·clud'ed
in·clu'/sion
in·clu'/sive
in·cog'/ni·to
in'co/her'/ent
in'com/bus'/ti/ble
in'come
in'com'/ing
in'com/men'/su/ra/ble
in'com/men'/su/rate
in'com/mode'
in'com/mu'/ni/ca/ble
in'com/mu'/ni/ca'do

in'com/mut'/a·ble
in·com'/pa/ra/ble
in'com/pat'i/bil'/i·ty
in'com/pat'/i·ble
in·com'/pe/tence
in'com/plete'
in'com/pre/hen'/si/ble
in'con/ceiv'/a·ble
in'con/clu'/sive
in'con/gru'/i·ty
(·ties)
in·con'/gru/ous
in·con'/se/quen'/tial
in'con/sid'/er/ate
in'con/sis'/ten·cy
(/cies)
in'con/sis'/tent
in'con/sol'/a·ble
in'con/spic'u/ous
in·con'/stan·cy
in·con'/stant
in'con/test'/a·ble
in'con/ve'/nient
in'con/vert'/i·ble
in·cor'/po/rate
in·cor'/po/ra'/tion
in'cor/po'/re·al
in'cor/rect'
in'cor/rect'ly
in·cor'/ri/gi/ble
in'cor/rupt'/i·ble
in·crease', *v.*
in'crease, *n.*
in·creas'/ing·ly
in·cred'i/bil'/i·ty
in·cred'/i·ble
in'cre/du'/li·ty
in·cred'u/lous
in'cre/ment
in·crim'i/nate
in·crim'i/na'/tion
in'cu/bate
in'cu/ba'/tion
in'cu/ba'/tor
in·cul'/cate
in·cum'/bent
in·cur'
in·cur'/a·ble
in·curred'
in·cur'/ring
in·debt'/ed/ness
in·de'/cen·cy (/cies)
in·de'/cent
in'·de/ci'/pher/a·ble
in'de/ci'/sion
in'de/ci'/sive
in'de/clin'/a·ble
in·deed'
in'de/fat'i/ga/ble
in'de/fen'/si/ble
in'de/fin'/a·ble
in·def'i/nite
in·del'/i·ble
in·del'i/ca·cy (/cies)

in·del'i/cate
in·dem'/ni/fi/ca'/tion
in·dem'/ni/fies
in·dem'/ni·fy
in·dem'/ni·ty (/ties)
in·dent'
in'den/ta'/tion
in·dent'ed
in·den'/tion
in·den'/ture
in·de/pen'/dence
in·de/struc'/ti/ble
in'de/ter'/mi/nate
in'de/ter'/mi/na/ble
in'dex (·dex·es;
·di/ces)
in'di/cate
in'di/ca'/tion
in·dic'a/tive
in·di'/ci·um (·a)
in·dict' (accuse)
in·dict'/ment
in·dif'/fer/ence
in·dif'/fer/ent·ly
in'/di/gence
in·dig'e/nous
in'di/gest'/i·ble
in'di/ges'/tion
in·dig'/nant
in'dig/na'/tion
in·dig'/ni·ty (/ties)
in'di·go (/gos)
in'di/rect'
in'dis/cern'/i·ble
in'dis/creet' (unwise)
in'dis/crete' (compact)
in'dis/cre'/tion
in'dis/crim'i/nate·ly
in'dis/pen'/sa/ble
in'dis/posed'
in'dis/po/si'/tion
in·dis/pu'/ta/ble
in'dis/sol'u/ble
in'dis/tinct'ly
in'dis/tin'/guish/a·ble
in·dite'
(put in writing)
in'di/vid'u·al
in'di/vid'u/al/ist
in'di/vid'u/al'/i·ty
(·ties)
in'di/vid'u/al·ly
in'di/vis'/i·ble
in'di/vis'i/bil'/i·ty
in·doc'/tri/nate
in·doc'/tri/na'/tion
in'do/lent
in·dom'i/ta/ble
in'doors'
in·dorse'
in'drawn'
in·du'/bi/ta/ble
in·duce'/ment
in·duct'

in·duc′/tion
in·duc′/tive
in·duc′/tor
in·dulge′
in·dul′/gence
in·dus′/tri·al
in·dus′/tri/al/ist
in·dus′/tri/al/ize
in·dus′/tri/ous
in′dus/try (/tries)
in·e′/bri/ate
in·e′/bri·a′/tion
in·ed′/i·ble
in·ef′/fa/ble
in′ef/face′/a·ble
in′ef/fec′/tive
in′ef/fec′/tu·al
in′ef/fi/ca′/cious
in·ef′/fi/ca·cy
in′ef/fi′/cien·cy
(/cies)
in′ef/fi′/cient
in·el′i/gi/bil′/i·ty
in·el′i/gi/ble
in·ept′
in·ep′/ti/tude
in′e·qual′/i·ty (·ties)
in·eq′/ui/ta/ble
in·eq′/ui·ty (/ties)
in·ert′
in·er′/tia
in′es/cap′/a·ble
in′es/sen′/tial
in·es′/ti/ma/ble
in·ev′i/ta/bil′/i·ty
in·ev′i/ta/ble
in′ex/act′
in′ex/cus′/a·ble
in′ex/haust′/i·ble
in·ex′o/ra/ble
in′ex/pen′/sive
in′ex/pe′/ri/enced
in·ex′/pert
in·ex′/pi/a·ble
in′ex/plain′/a·ble
in·ex/pli′/ca/ble
in′ex/plic′it
in′ex/press′/i·ble
in′ex/pres′/sive
in′ex/ten′/si/ble
in′ex/tin′/guish/a·ble
in·ex/tri′/ca/ble
in·fal′/li/ble
in′fa/mous
in′fa·my (/mies)
in′fan·cy (/cies)
in′fant
in′fan/tile
in′fan/til/ism
in′fan/try (/tries)
in·fat′u/ate
in·fat′u/a′tion
in·fect′
in·fec′/tion

in·fec'/tious
in·fer'
in'fer/ence
in·fe'/ri·or
in·fe'/ri/or'/i·ty (·ties)
in·fer'/nal
in·fer'no (/nos)
in·ferred'
in·fer'/ring
in·fest'
in'fes/ta'/tion
in'fi/del
in'fi/del'/i·ty (·ties)
in'field'er
in·fil'/trate
in'fil/tra'/tion
in'fi/nite
in'fin·i/tes'i/mal
in·fin'i/tive
in·fin'i·ty(·ties)
in·firm'
in·fir'/ma·ry (/ries)
in·fir'/mi·ty (/ties)
in·flame'
in·flamed'
in·flam'/ma/ble
in'flam/ma'/tion
in·flam'/ma/to'ry
in·flate'
in·flat'ed
in·fla'/tion
in·fla'/tion/ar'y
in·flec'/tion
in·flex'/i·ble
in·flict'
in·flic'/tion
in'flu/ence
in'flu/en'/tial
in'flu/en'za
in'flux
in·form'
in·for'/mal
in'for/mal'/i·ty (·ties)
in·for'/mant
in'for/ma'/tion
in·for'/ma/tive
in·frac'/tion
in'fra/red'
in·fre'/quent
in·fringe'
in·fu'/ri/ate
in·fuse'
in·fu'/sion
in·ge'/nious
in'gé'/nue'
in'ge/nu'/i·ty (·ties)
in·glo'/ri/ous
in'got
in·grained'
in'grate
in·gra'/ti/ate
in·gra'/ti/at'/ing·ly
in·grat'i/tude

in·gre'/di/ent
in'grown'
in·hab'it
in·hab'/it/a·ble
in·hab'i/tant
in'ha/la'/tion
in'ha/la'/tor
in·hale'
in·her'/ent
in·her'it
in·her'i/tance
in·hib'it
in'hi/bi'/tion
in·hos/pi'/ta/ble
in·hu'/man
in'hu/mane'
in·im'/i·cal
in·im'i/ta/ble
in·iq'/ui·ty (/ties)
in·i'/tial
in·i'/ti/ate
in·i'/ti·a'/tion
in·ject'
in·jec'/tion
in'ju/di'/cious
in·junc'/tion
in'jure
in'jur/ing
in·ju'/ri/ous
in'ju·ry (/ries)
in·jus'/tice
ink'/ling
ink'y
in·laid'
in'land
in·lay', *v.*
in'let
in'mate
in me·mo'/ri·am
in'most
in'nate·ly
in'ner
in'ner/most
in'ning
in'no/cence
in·noc'u/ous
in'no/vate
in'no/va'/tion
in·nu'/mer/a·ble
in·nu'/mer/ous
in·oc'u/late
in·oc'u/la'/tion
in'of/fen'/sive
in·op'/er/a·ble
in·op'/por/tune'
in·or'/di/nate
in'or/gan'ic
in'put'
in'quest
in·quire'
in·quir'y (/ies)
in'qui/si'/tion
in·quis'i/tive
in'road'

in·sane′
in·san′i/tar′y
in·san′/i·ty (·ties)
in·sa′/ti/a·ble
in·scribe′
in·scrip′/tion
in·scru′/ta/ble
in′sect
in·sec′/ti/cide
in′se/cure′
in′se/cu′/ri·ty (/ties)
in·sen′/si/ble
in·sen′/si/tive
in·sep′a/ra/ble
in·sert′, *v.*
in′sert, *n.*
in·ser′/tion
in′set′
in′side′
in·sid′i/ous
in′sight′
in·sig′/ni·a, *pl.*
(*sing.*·sig′·ne)
in′sig/nif′i/cant
in′sin/cere′
in′sin/cer′/i·ty (·ties)
in·sin′u/ate
in·sin′u/a′tion
in·sip′id
in·sist′
in·sis′/tent
in′so/far′ as
in′so/lence
in·sol′u/ble
in·solv′/a·ble
in·sol′/ven·cy
in·sol′/vent
in·som′/ni·a
in·spect′
in·spec′/tion
in·spec′/tor
in′spi/ra′/tion
in·spire′
in′sta/bil′/i·ty
in′stal/la′/tion
in/stalled′
in·stall′/ment
in′stance
in′stan/ta′/ne/ous
in′stant·ly
in·stead′
in′step
in′sti/gate
in′sti/ga′/tor
in·still′
in·stilled′
in·stinct′, *adj.*
in′stinct, *n.*
in·stinc′/tive
in′sti/tute
in′sti/tu′/tion
in·struct′
in·struct′ed
in·struc′/tion

ı·struc'/tor
ı'stru/ment
ı'stru/men'/tal
ı'sub/or'/di/nate
ı'sub/or'/di/na'/tion
ı·suf'/fer/a·ble
ı'suf/fi'/cient
ı'su/late
ı'su/la'/tion
ı'su/lin
ı·sult', *v.*
ı'sult, n.
ı·sur'/a·ble
ı·sur'/ance
ı·sure'
ı·sur'/gent
ı'sur/mount'/a·ble
ı'sur/rec'/tion
ı·tact'
ı·ta'/glio (/glios)
ı'take'
ı·tan'/gi/ble
ı'te/ger
ı'te/gral
ı'te/grate
ı'te/gra'/tion
ı·teg'/ri·ty
ı'tel/lect
ı'tel/lec'/tu·al
ı·tel'/li/gence
 quo'/tient (I.Q.)
ı·tel'/li/gent'/si·a
in·tel'/li/gi/ble
in·tem'/per/ance
in·tem'/per/ate
in·tend'
in·tense'
in·ten'/si/fies
in·ten'/si·fy
in·ten'/si·ty (/ties)
in·ten'/sive
in·tent'
in·ten'/tion/al·ly
in·ter' (bury)
in'ter/cede'
in'ter/cept'
in'ter/ces'/sion
in'ter/ces'/so·ry
in'ter/course
in'ter/de/pen'/dent
in'ter/est
in'ter/fere'
in'ter/fer'/ence
in'ter/fer'/ing
in'ter·im
in·te'/ri·or
in'ter/ject'
in'ter/jec'/tion
in'ter/leave'
in'ter/lop'er
in'ter/lude
in'ter/mar'/riage
in'ter/me'/di/ate
in·ter'/ment

in·ter′/mi/na/ble
in′ter/mis′/sion
in′ter/mit′/tent
in′tern, *n.*
in·tern′, *v.*
in·ter′/nal
in′ter/na′/tion·al
in′ter/plan′e/tar′y
in·ter′/po/late
in′ter/pose′
in·ter′/pret
in·ter′/pre/ta′/tion
in·terred′
in·ter′/ring
in·ter′/ro/gate
in·ter′/ro/ga′/tion
in′ter/rog′a/tive
in′ter/rupt′
in′ter/rup′/tion
in′·ter/scho/las′/tic
in′ter/sect′
in′ter/sec′/tion
in′ter/sperse′
in′ter/state′
in′ter/val
in′ter/vene′
in′ter/ven′/tion
in′ter/view
in·tes′/tate
in·tes′/ti/nal
in·tes′/tine
in′ti/ma·cy (/cies)
in′ti/mate
in′ti/ma′/tion
in·tim′i/date
in·tim′i/da′/tion
in·tol′/er/a·ble
in·tol′/er/ance
in′to/na′/tion
in·tox′i/cate
in·tox′i/ca′/tion
in′tra/mu′/ral
in·tran′/si/tive
in′tra/state
in′tra/ve′/nous
in·trench′
in·trep′id
in′tri/ca·cy (/cies)
in′tri/cate
in·trigue′
in·tri′/guing
in·trin′/sic
in′tro/duce′
in′tro/duc′/tion
in′tro/duc′/to·ry
in′tro/spec′/tion
in′tro/vert′, *v.*
in′tro/vert′, *n.*
in·trude′
in·tru′/sion
in′tu·i′/tion
in·tu′i/tive
in′un/date
in′un/da′/tion

n·ure'
n·vade'
n·val'id (void)
n'va/lid (ill person)
n·val'i/date
n·val'u/a·ble
n·var'i/a·ble
n·va'/sion
n·vec'/tive
n·vei'/gle
n·vent'
n·ven'/tion
n·ven'/tor
n'ven/to'ry (/ries)
n·verse'
n·ver'/sion
n·vert', *v.*
n'vert, *adj., n.*
n·vest'
n·ves'/ti/gate
n·ves'/ti/ga'/tion
n·vest'/ment
n·ves'/tor
n·vet'/er/ate
n·vig'/or/ate
n·vin'/ci/ble
n·vi'o/la/ble
n·vis'/i·ble
n'vi/ta'/tion
n·vite'
n·vit'/ing
in'vo/ca'/tion
in'voice
in·voke'
in·vol'/un/tar'y
in·volve'
in·volv'/ing
in·vul'/ner/a·ble
in'ward·ly
i'o·dine
i·o'ta
i·ras'/ci/ble
i'rate
ir'i/des'/cence
irk'/some
i'ron/clad'
i·ron'/i·cal
i'ro·ny (/nies)
ir·ra'/di/ate
ir·ra'/tion·al
ir·rec'/on/cil'/a·ble
ir're/deem'/a·ble
ir're/duc'/i·ble
ir·re/fut'/a·ble
ir·reg'u/lar
ir·rel'a/tive
ir·rel'e/vance
ir're/li'/gious
ir·re/me'/di/a·ble
ir·rep'a/ra/ble
ir're/place'/a·ble
ir're/press'/i·ble
ir're/proach'/a·ble
ir're/sist'/i·ble

ir·res'o/lute
ir're/spec'/tive
ir're/spon'/si/ble
ir're/spon'/sive
ir're/triev'/a·ble
ir·rev'/er/ent
ir're/vers'/i·ble
ir/rev'o/ca/ble
ir'ri/gate
ir'ri/ga'/tion
ir'ri/ta/ble
ir'ri/tate
ir'ri/ta'/tion
ir·rup'/tion (invasion)
is'land
i'so/late
i'so/la'/tion
i'so/la'/tion/ist
is'su/ance
is'sue
i·tal'/ic
i·tal'i/cize
i'tem/ize
i·tin'/er/ant
i·tin'/er/ar'y (/ies)
its
it's (it is)
i'vo·ry (/ries)
i'vy (·vies)

J

jack'et
jack'/knife' (/knives')
jack/pot
jag'/ged
ja·lop'y (/ies)
jammed
jam'/bo/ree'
jan'i/tor
Jap'a/nese'
jar'/gon
jarred
jar'/ring
jas'/mine
jas'/per
jaun'/dice
jaun'/ti·ly
jaunt'y
jay'/walk'/ing
jeal'/ous
jeer'/ing·ly
jel'/lied
jeop'/ard/ize
jeop'/ard·y
jerk'i·ly

erk'y
er'/sey (/seys)
est'/ing · ly
Jes'u · it
jet'/sam
jet'/ti/son
jet'ty (/ties)
jew'el
jew'/eled
jew'/el · er
jew'/el · ry
jif'fy (/fies)
jig'/ger
jig'/gle
jilt'ed
jin'/gle
jinx
jit'/ter/bug'
jit'/ters, *pl.*
job'/ber
jock'ey (/eys)
John'/ston, R. I.
Johns'/town, N. Y., Pa.
join'er
joint'ly
joist
jok'/ing · ly
jol'ly
jon'/quil
jos'/tle
jot'/ting
jour'/nal
jour'/nal/ism
jour'/nal/ist
jour'/ney (/neys)
jour'/neyed
jour'/ney/man (/men)
jo'vi · al
joy'/ful · ly
joy'/ous/ness
ju'bi/lant
ju'bi/la'/tion
ju'bi/lee
judg'/ing
judg'/ment
ju'di/ca/to'ry
ju · di'/cial
ju · di'/ci/ar'y (/ies)
ju · di'/cious
jug'/gler
jug'u/lar
juic'i/ness
juic'y
ju · jit'su
juke'/box'
ju'lep
jum'/ble
jum'bo (/bos)
jump'er
junc'/tion
junc'/ture
jun'/gle
jun'/ior
ju'ni/per

ju'ris/dic'/tion
ju'ris/pru'/dence
ju'rist
ju'ror
ju'ry (ries)
ju'ry/man (/men)
jus'/tice
jus'/ti/fi'/a · ble
jus'/ti/fi/ca'/tion
jus'/ti/fied
jus'/ti · fy
ju've/nile
jux'/ta/po/si'/tion

K

kai'/ser
kan'/ga/roo' (/roos')
ka'pok
kar'a/kul
Kear'/ney, Nebr.
Kear'ny, N. J.
keel
keen'/ness
keep'/sake'
ken'/nel
ker'/nel
ker'o/sine'
ket'/tle/drum'
key'/board'
keyed
key'/hole'
key'/note'
key'/stone'
kha'ki
ki'bitz · er
kick'/back'
kick'/off'
kid'/nap
kid'/naped
kid'/ney (/neys)
kill'er
kill'/joy
kiln
kil'o/cy'/cle
kil'o/gram
ki · lo'/me/ter
kil'o/watt'
kil'o · watt'—/hour'
kilt
ki · mo' · no (/nos)
kin'/der/gar'/ten
kind'/heart'ed
kin'/dle
kind'li/ness
kin'/dling

kin'/dred
king'/dom
kink'y
kink'i/ness
kins'/folk', *pl.*
kip'/per
kis'/met
kiss'/ing
kitch'en
kitch'/en/ette'
kitch'/en/ware'
kit'/ten/ish
klep'/to/ma'/ni·a
klep'/to/ma'/ni·ac
knack
knap'/sack'
knead
knee'/cap'
knick'/knack'
knife (knives)
knit
knit'/ting
knock'/down'
knock'/out'
knot'ty
know'—/how', *n.*
know'/ing·ly
knowl'/edge
knowl'/edge/a·ble
knuck'le
Ko'dak
ko'sher
kow'/tow'
kraft (paper)
krem'/lin
Ku Klux Klan
kum'/quat

L

la'bel
la'beled
la'bel/ing
la'bor
lab'o/ra/to'ry (/ries)
la'bor·er
la·bo'/ri/ous
lab'y/rinth
lac'/er/ate
lac/er·a'/tion
lach'/ry/mal
lack'a/dai'/si/cal
Lack'a/wan·na, N. Y.
la·con'ic
lac'/quer
la·crosse'

lad'/der
lad'/ing
la'dle
la'dy/like'
La'fay/ette', Ind.
lag'/gard
la·goon'
lais·sez—/faire'
la'i·ty
la·ment'
la'men/ta/ble
lam'/en/ta'/tion
lam'i/nate
lamp'/black
lam/poon'
la·nai'
land'/fall'
land'/la'dy (/dies)
land'/locked'
land'/lord'
land'/lub'/ber
land'/mark'
land'/scape
lan'/guage
lan'/guid
lan'/guish
lan'/guor
lan'o/lin
Lan'/sing, Mich.
lan'/tern
la·pel'
lap'i/dar'y (/ies)
lapse
lar'/ce/nous
lar'/ce·ny (/nies)
large'ly
lar/gess'
lar'go
lar'va (/vae)
lar'/yn/gi'/tis
lar'/ynx (la·ryn'/ges; /ynx·es)
las/civ'i/ous
las'/si/tude
Las'tex
late'ly
late'/ness
la'tent
lat'er
lat'/er·al
lat'/est
lathe
Lat'in
lat'i/tude
la·trine'
lat'/ter
lat'/tice
laud'/a·ble
lau'/da/num
lau'/da/to'ry
laugh'/a·ble
laugh'/ter
launch
laun'/der

laun'/dry (/dries)
lau'/re/ate
lau'/rel
lav'a/to'ry (/ries)
lav'/en/der
lav'/ish
law'—/a·bid'ing
law'/ful
law'/less
law'/mak'er
law'/mak'/ing
law'/suit'
law'/yer
lax'a/tive
lax'/i·ty
lay'/man (/men)
lay'/off'
lay'/out'
la'zi/ness
lead, *v.* (to guide)
lead, *n.* (a metal)
lead'/er/ship
leaf (leaves)
leaf'/let
league
League of Na'tions
leak'/age
lean'/ness
leap'/frog'
learned, *v.*
learn'ed, *adj.*
lease
leased
leath'er
leav'en
lech'/er/ous
lec'/tern
lec'/ture
lec'/tur·er
ledge
ledg'er
leech
lee'/way'
left'—/hand'ed
leg'a·cy (/cies)
le'gal
le·gal'/i·ty (·ties)
le'gal/ize
le'gal·ly
leg'a/tee'
le·ga'/tion
le·ga'to
leg'/end
le'g/en/dar'y
leg'/er/de/main'
leg'i/bil'/i·ty
leg'/i·ble
le'gion
le'gion/naire'
leg'/is/late
leg'/is/la'/tion
leg'/is/la'/tive
leg'/is/la'/tor
leg'/is/la'/ture

le·git'i/ma·cy
le·git'i/mate
leg'/ume
lei'/sure
lem'on
lem'/on/ade'
lend'—/lease'
length'/wise'
length'y
le'nience
le'nient
Len'/in/grad'
Len'/in/ism
len'/til
leop'/ard
le'o/tard
lep'/re/chaun
lep'/ro·sy
lep'/rous
le'sion
les/see'
less'en, *v.*
less'er
les'/son, *n.*
les'/sor
le'thal
le·thar'/gic
leth'/ar·gy (/gies)
let'/ter
let'/tered
let'/ter/head'
let'/ter/press'
let'/tuce
let'up, *n.*
leu/ke'/mi·a
Le·vant'
lev'el
lev'/eled
le'ver/age
le·vi'a/than
lev'i/ta'/tion
lev'/i·ty (·ties)
lex'i/con
li'a/bil'/i·ty (·ties)
li'a/ble
li'ai/son
li'bel
li'bel/ous
lib'/er·al
lib'/er/al'/i·ty (·ties)
lib'/er/al/ize
lib'/er/al·ly
lib'/er/ate
lib'/er·a'/tion
lib'/er·a'/tor
lib'/er·ty (/ties)
li·brar'i·an
li'brary (/ies)
li·bra'/tion
li·bret'/tist
li·bret'to
(/tos; ·bret·ti)
li'cense
li'cen/see'

i·cen'/tious
i'chen
ic'it
ic'o/rice
ien (claim)
ieu
ieu/ten'/an·cy
ieu/ten'/ant
life belt
life'/blood'
life'/boat
life buoy
life'/guard'
life'/less
life'/like'
life'/long'
life'/sav'er
life'/time'
lift'/ing
lig'a/ment
li·ga'/tion
lig'a/ture
light'/en/ing
(relieving)
light'/ning
(atmospheric electricity)
light'/weight'
lig'/nite
lik'/a·ble
like'/li/hood
like'ly
like'/ness

like'/wise'
lik/ing
li'lac
lil'·y (/ies)
lim'/ber
lime'/light'
Lim'/er/ick
lime'/stone'
lim'i/ta'/tion
lim'/it·ed
lim'/it/less
lim'/ou/sine'
lim'/pid
Lin'/coln
lin'e/age
lin'e·al
lin'e/a·ment (feature)
lin'e·ar
line'/man (/men)
lin'en
lines'/man (/men)
lin'/ger
lin'/ge/rie
lin'go (/goes)
lin'/gual
lin'/guist
lin'i/ment (an oil)
lin'/ing
link'/age
li·no'/le·um
Lin'o/type
lin'/seed'

li'on/ess
lip'/stick'
liq'/ue/fied
liq'/ue/fy'/ing
li · queur'
liq'/uid
liq'/ui/date
liq'/ui/da'/tion
liq'/uor
lis'/some
lis'/ten
Lis/ter/ine'
list'/less
lit'a · ny (/nies)
lit'/er · a · cy
lit'/er · al
lit'/er/al · ly
lit'/er/ar'y
lit'/er · a/ture
lithe
lithe'/some
lith'o/graph
li · thog'/ra/pher
li · thog'/ra/phy
Lith'u/a'ni · an
lit'i/gant
lit'i/gate
lit'i/ga'/tion
lit'/mus
lit'/ter
lit'/tle
li · tur'/gi/cal
lit'/ur · gy (/gies
liv'/a · ble
live'/li/hood
live'/long'
liv'/er/wurst'
liv'/er · y/man (/men)
live'/stock'
liz'/ard
liv'id
liv'/ing
load'/ing
loaf (loaves)
loam (a soil)
loan
loath (reluctant)
loathe (to dislike)
lob'/by (/bies)
lob'/by/ist
lob'/ster
lo'cal
lo · cale'
lo · cal'/i · ty (· ties)
lo'cal/ize
lo'cal · ly
lo · ca'/tion
lock'/out'
lock'/smith'
lo'co/mo'/tion
lo'co/mo'/tive
lo'cust
lo · cu'/tion
lodg'/ing

oft'y
og'a/rithm
oge
og'ic
og'/i·cal
o·gi'/cian
o·gis'/tics
og'/roll'/ing
Lo'hen/grin
loi'/ter
lol'/li/pop
lone'/li/ness
lone'ly
lone'/some
lon/gev'/i·ty
long'/hand
lon'/gi/tude
lon'/gi/tu'/di/nal
long'—/lived'
long'—/play'ing (LP)
long'/shore'/man
(/men)
look'/ing glass
look'/out'
loop'/hole'
loose (unattached)
loose'ly
lop'/sid'ed
lo·qua'/cious
Lor'e/lei
lor'/gnette'
Los Al'a/mos
Los An'ge/les, Calif.
los'/a·ble
lose (incur loss)
los'/ing
lo'tion
lot'/ter·y (/ies)
Lou'i/si/an'a
Lou'/is/ville
lou'/ver
lov'/a·ble
love'/li/ness
love'/lorn'
love'ly
love'/sick'
lov'ing—/kind'ness
low'—/down', *adj.*
low'/down', *n.*
Low'/ell
low'/land
low'/li/ness
loy'al
loy'/al·ty (/ties)
loz'/enge
lu'bri/cant
lu'bri/cate
lu'bri/ca'/tion
lu'cid
lu·cid'/i·ty
luck·i·ly
luck'y
lu'cra/tive
lu'di/crous

lug'/gage
lu·gu'/bri/ous
luke'/warm'
lul'/a·by (/bies)
lum/ba'go
lum'/bar (pert. to loins)
lum'/ber (timber)
lum'/ber
(move clumsily)
lu'mi/nar'y (/ies)
lu'mi/nous
lu'na·cy (/cies)
lu'na/tic
lun'/cheon
lu'pine
lurch
lu'rid

lus'/cious
lus'/ter
lust'/ful
lus'/trous
Lu'ther·an
lux·u'/ri/ant
lux·u'/ri/ate
lux·u/ri/ous
lux'u·ry (/ries)
ly·ce'um
ly'ing
lym/phat'ic
lynch
lynx
ly'on/naise'
lyr'ic
lyr'/i·cal

M

ma-ca'/bre
mac/ad'am
mac/ad'/am/ize
mac'a/ro'ni
mac'a/roon'
Mac/Ar'/thur
Ma·cau'/lay
Mac/beth'
Mac'e/do'/ni·a
mac'/er/ate

mac'/er·a'/tion
mach'i/na'/tion
ma·chine'
ma·chin'/er·y
ma·chin'/ist
mack'/er·el
mack'/in/tosh
(raincoat)
mad'am (mes'/dames')
ma'de/moi'/selle'

Ma·dei'ra
ma·dras'
mad'/ri/gal
mag'a/zine'
Ma·gel'/lan
mag'/got
mag'ic
ma·gi'/cian
Ma·gi/not
mag'/is/te'/ri·al
mag'/is/trate
Mag'na Char'ta
mag'/na/nim'/i·ty (·ties)
mag/nan'i/mous
mag'/nate (person of rank)
mag/ne'/sia
mag/ne'/si·um
mag'/net (that which attracts)
mag/net'ic
mag'/ne/tize
mag/ne'to (/tos)
mag'/ni/fi/ca'/tion
mag/nif'i/cence
mag/nif'i/cent
mag'/ni/fi'er
mag'/ni/fy'/ing
mag/nil'o/quent
mag'/ni/tude
mag/no'/li·a
mag'/pie
Mag'/yar
ma·ha'/ra'ja
Mah'—/Jongg'
ma·hog'a·ny (/nies)
maid'en
maid'/en·hair' (fern)
maid'/en·ly
maid'/ser/vant'
mail'/a·ble
mail'/man'
mail'—/order house
main'/land
main'ly
main'/mast'
main'/spring'
main'/stay'
main/tain'
main'/te/nance
maî'/tre d'hô'/tel'
maize (corn)
ma·jes'/tic
maj'/es·ty (/ties)
ma'jor
ma'jor/do'mo (/mos)
ma'jo/rette'
ma'jor gen'/er·al
ma·jor'/i·ty (·ties)
make'—/be·lieve', *adj., n.*
make'/fast'

M

make'/shift'
make'up, *n.*
make'/weight'
mak'/ing
mal'/ad/just'/ment
mal'/ad/min'/is/ter
mal'a/droit'
mal'a · dy (/dies)
ma · laise'
mal'/ap/ro/pos'
ma · lar'i · a
Ma · lay'
mal'/con/tent'
mal'e/dic'/tion
mal'e/fac'/tor
ma · lef'ic
ma · lef'i/cent
ma · lev'o/lence
mal/fea'/sance
mal'/for/ma'/tion
mal/formed'
mal'/ice
ma · li'/cious
ma · lign'
ma · lig'/nan · cy
ma · lig'/nant
ma · lign'er
(one who injures)
ma · lin'/ger
(feign illness)
mal'/lard
mal'/le · a/bil'/i · ty
mal'/le/a · ble
mal'/let
mal'/low
mal'/nu/tri'/tion
mal/o'dor
mal/o'dor/ous
mal'/po/si'/tion
mal'/prac'/tice
Mal'/tese'
Mal/thu'/sian
malt'/ose
mal/treat'
mam'ma
mam'/mal
mam'/mon
mam'/moth
man'/a · cle
man'/age
man'/age/a · ble
man'/age/ment
man'/ag · er
man'a/ge'/ri · al
Man'/ches/ter
Man/chu'/ri · an
man/da'/mus
man'/da/rin
man'/date
man'/da/tor · y
man'/di/ble
man/do/lin'
man'/drel
man'—/eat'er

ma•nege′
ma•neu′/ver
ma•neu/ver•a/bil′-/i•ty
man′/ga/nese
man′/ger
man′/gle
man′/grove
man′/han′/dle
man′/hole
man′/hood
ma′ni•a
ma′ni•ac
ma•ni′/a•cal
man′i/cure
man′i/fest
man′i/fes/ta′/tion
man′i/fold
Ma•nil′a
ma•nip′u/late
ma•nip′u/la/to′ry
Man′i/to′ba
man′/kind′
man′na
man′/ne/quin
man′/ner
man′/ner/ism
man′—/of—/war′
(men′— . . .)
man′or
man′/pow′er
man′/sion
man′/slaugh′/ter
man′/tel/piece′
man/til′la
man′/tle (cloak)
man′u•al
man′u/fac′/ture (/tur/ing)
ma•nure′
man′u/script
man′y—/sid′ed
man′/za/ni′ta
mar′a/bou
ma•ra′ca
mar′a/schi′no
mar′a/thon
ma•raud′
mar′/ble
mar′/ble/ize
mar/che′se
Mar/co′ni
Mar′di Gras′
mar′/ga/rine
mar′/gin•al
mar′/gue/rite′
mar′i/gold
mar′i/jua′na
ma•rim′ba
mar′i/nate
ma•rine′
mar′i/ner
mar′i/o•nette′
mar′i/tal
mar′i/time

mar′/jo/ram
marked
mark′/ed·ly
mar′/ket
mar′/ket/a·ble
mar′/ket/ing
marks′/man (/men)
mark′up
mar′/lin
mar′/ma/lade
mar′/mo/set
mar′/mot
ma·roon′
marque
mar/quee′
mar/quis′, *masc.*
mar/quise′, *fem.*
mar′/qui/sette′
mar′/riage
mar′/riage/a·ble
mar′/ried
mar′/row
Mar′/seil/laise′
Mar/seilles′
mar′/shal (official)
marsh′/mal′/low
mar/su′/pi·al
mar′/ten (animal)
mar′/tial (military)
mar′/tin (bird)
mar′/ti/net′
mar′/tyr
mar′/tyr/dom
mar′/vel
mar′/vel/ous
Marx′i·an
Marx′/ism
mas/car′a
mas′/cot
mas′/cu/line
mash′ie
ma′son
Ma·son′ic
Ma′son/ite
ma′son·ry (/ries)
masque
mas′/quer/ade′
Mas′/sa/chu′/setts
mas′/sa/cre
mas/sage′
mas/seur′, *masc.*
mas/seuse′, *fem.*
mas′/sive
mas′/ter/dom
mas′/ter/ful
mas′/ter·ly
mas′/ter/piece′
mas′/ter·y (/ies)
mast′/head′
mas′/tic
mas′/ti/cate
mas′/ti/ca/to′ry
mas′/tiff
mas′/to/don

mas'/toid
mat'a/dor
match'/board'
match'/less
match'/mak'er
ma·te'/ri·al
(pert. to matter)
ma·te'/ri/al/ism
ma·te'/ri/al/is'/tic
ma·te'/ri/al·ly
ma·té'/ri·el'
(equipment)
ma·ter'/nal
ma·ter'/ni·ty (/ties)
math'e/mat'/i·cal
math'e/ma/ti'/cian
math'e/mat'/ics
mat'i/nee'
mat'/ing
mat'/rass (glass vessel)
ma'tri/arch
ma'tri/arch'y
ma'tri/cide
ma·tric'u/late
ma'tric·u/la'/tion
mat'/ri/mo'/ni·al
mat'/ri/mo·ny
ma'trix (·tri/ces)
ma'tron
ma'tron/age
ma'tron/li/ness
mat'/ter
mat'ter—/of—/course',
adj.
Mat'/thew
mat'/ting
mat'/tock
mat'/toid
mat'/tress (bed)
mat'u/rate
mat'u/ra'/tion
ma·tured'
ma·tu'/ri·ty
maud'/lin
maul
maun'/der
mau'/so/le'um (/ums;
/le'a)
mauve
mav'/er/ick
mawk'/ish
max'im
max'i/mal
Max'i/mil'/lian
max'i/mize
max'i/mum
may be, *v*
may'be, *adv.*
May Day
May'/flow'er
may'/hap'
may'/hem
may'/on/naise'
may'or

may'/or/al·ty
May'/pole'
maze (a puzzle)
ma·zur'ka
Mc'In/tosh (apple)
mead'ow
mea/ger
meal'/time'
mealy/mouthed'
mean
me·an'/der
mean'/ing
mean'ly
mean'/ness
mean'/time'
mean'/while'
mea'/sles
mea'/sur/a·ble
mea'/sure/ment
mea'/sur/ing
Mec'ca
me·chan'ic
me·chan'/i·cal
mech'a/nism
med'al (a reward)
med'/al/ist
me·dal'/lion
med'/dle (interfere)
med'/dler
med'/dle/some
me'di·an
me'di/ate
me'di·a'/tion
med'ic
med'/i·cal
med'i/cate
med'i/ca'/tion
me·dic'i/nal
med'i/cine
me'di·e'/val
me'di·o'/cre
me'di/oc'/ri·ty (/ties)
med'i/tate
med'i/ta'/tion
Med'i/ter/ra'/ne·an
me'di·um (/ums; ·di·a)
med'/ley
Me·du'sa
meet'/ing
meg'a/phone
mel'/an/cho'/li·a
mel'/an/chol'y
Mel'/bourne
Mel/chiz'e/dek
meld
me·lee'
me'/lio/rate
me'lio/ra'/tion
mel/lif'/lu/ence
mel'/low
me·lod'ic
me·lo'/di/ous
mel'o/dra'ma

nel'o · dy (/dies)
nel'on
nem'/ber/ship
nem'/brane
ne · men'to (/tos)
nem'/oirs
nem'o/ra/ble
nem'o/ran'/dum
(/dums; · da)
me · mo'/ri · al
mem'o/riz/ing
mem'o · ry (/ries)
Mem'/phis
men'/ace
me · nag'/er · ie
men/da'/cious
men/dac'/i · ty
Men/de'/lian
Men'/dels/sohn
men'/di/cant
me'nial
men'/in/gi'/tis
Men'/non/ite
men'o/pause
men'/stru · al
men'/stru · a'/tion
men'/su/ra · ble
men'/tal
men/tal'/i · ty (· ties)
men'/thol
men'/tioned
men'u
Men'u/hin
Meph/is/toph'e/les
mer'/can/tile
mer'/ce/nar'y
mer'/cer/ized
mer'/chan/dise
mer'/chant
mer'/chant/a · ble
mer'/chant/man
(/men)
mer'/ci/ful
mer'/ci/less
mer/cu'/ri · al
Mer/cu'/ro/chrome'
Mer'/cu · ry
mer'cy (/cies)
mere'ly
mer'e/tri'/cious
merg'er
me · rid'i · an
me · ringue'
me · ri'no (/nos)
mer'it
mer'i/to'/ri/ous
mer'/maid'
mer'/ri · ly
mer'/ri/ment
mer'ry
mer'ry—/go—/round'
mer'/ry/mak'/ing
me'sa
mes'/dames', *pl.*

mesh'/work
mes'/mer/ism
mes'/mer/ize
Mes'o/po/ta'/mi·a
mes/quite'
mes'/sage
mes'/sa/line
mes'/sen/ger
Mes/si'ah
mes'/sieurs, *pl.*
mess'y
met'a/bol'ic
me·tab'o/lism
met'a/car'/pus (pi)
met'al
me·tal'/lic
met'/al/lur·gy
met'a/mor'/pho/sis (/ses)
met'a/phor
met'a/phys'/ics
met'a/tar'/sus (·si)
mete
me'te·or
me'te/or'ic
me'te/or/ite
me'te/or/ol'o·gy
me'ter
me'thod'/i·cal
Meth'/od/ist
meth'/od/ol'o·gy
Me·thu'/se/lah
meth'yl
me·tic'u/lous
me·ton'y·my
met'/ric
met'/ro/nome
me·trop'o/lis
met'/ro/pol'i/tan
met'/tle/some
Mex'i/can
mez'/za/nine
mez'zo /so·pra'no (/nos)
Mi·am'i
Mi'chel/an'/ge·lo
Mich'i/gan
mi'cro/a·nal'y/sis(/ses
mi'crobe
Mi'cro/card
mi'cro/film
mi'cro/groove
mi·crom'e/ter
mi'crons
mi'cro/phone
mi'cro/scop'ic
mi'cro/wave
mic'/tu·rate
mid'/day
mid'/dle/man (/men)
midg'et
mid'/night
mid'/riff
mid'/ship/men

nid'/sum'/mer
nid'/way'
nid'/wife' (/wives')
nien
night'y
ni'gnon/ette'
ni'graine
mi'grant
mi'grate
mi·gra'/tion
mi'gra/to'ry
mi·ka'do
mi·la'dy
mil'/dew
mild'ly
mild'/ness
mile'/age
mile'/post'
mile'/stone'
mil'i/tan·cy
mil'i/tant
mil'i/ta/rism
mil'i/ta/rist
mil'i/tar'y
mi·li'/tia
mi·li'/tia/man (/men)
milk'er
milk'i/ness
milk'/man' (/men')
milk'weed'
mil/len'/ni·um
(/ums; /ni·a)
mill'er
mil'/li/ner'y
mil'/lion
mil'/lion/aire'
mil'/lionth
mill'/pond'
mill'/stone'
mill'/wright'
Mil/wau'/kee
mim'e/o·graph
mi·me'/sis
mim'ic
mim'/icked
mim'/ic·ry
min'a/ret'
mince'/meat'
mince pie
minc'/ing·ly
mind'/ful
min'er (one who mines)
min'/er/al'/o·gy
min'/er/al/og/i·cal
Mi·ner'va
mi·ne/stro'ne
min'/gle
min'i/a·ture
min'i/mal
min'i/mize
min'i/mum
min'/ing
min'/ion
min'/is/ter

min′/is/te′/ri · al
min′/is/tra′/tion
min′/is/try (/tries)
Min′/ne/ap′o/lis
Min′/ne/so′ta
min′/now
mi′nor (lesser)
mi · nor′/i · ty (· ties)
min′/strel
min′u/end
min′u · et′
mi′nus
min′/ute, *n. & v.*
mi · nute′, *adj.*
min′/ute · ly (continually)
mi · nute′ly (in detail)
mir′/a · cle
mi · rac′u/lous
mi · rage′
mir′/ror
mirth′/less
mis′/ad/ven′/ture
mis′al/li′/ance
mis′/an/thrope
mis′ap/pre/hen′/sion
mis′/ap/pro′/pri/ate
mis′/be/got′/ten
mis′/be/have′
mis′/be/lieve′
mis/cal′/cu/late
mis′/cal/cu/la′/tion
mis/car′/riage
mis′/ce/ge/na′/tion
mis′/cel/la′/ne/ous
mis′/cel/la′ny (/nies)
mis′/chief
mis′/chie/vous
mis/con/ceive′
mis′/con/cep′/tion
mis/con′/duct
mis′/con/strue′
mis′/cre/ant
mis′/de/mean′or
mis′/er/a · ble
mi · se/re′re
mi′ser/li/ness
mis′/er · y (/ies)
mis/fea′/sance
mis/fit′
mis/for′/tune
mis/giv′/ing
mis/hap′
mis′/in/ter′/pret · ed
mis/judge′
mis/judg′/ment
mis/laid′
mis/man′/age
mis/no′/mer
mis/place′
mi · sog′a/mist
mis′/pro/nounce′
mis′/quo/ta′/tion
mis′/rep/re/sen/ta′-
/tion

is/rule′
issed
iss′es
is/shap′en
is′/sile
is′/sion
is′/sion/ar′y (/ies)
lis′/sis/sip′pi
is′/sive
Mis/sou′ri
nis/spell′
nis/spend′
nis/state′/ment
nis/tak′/a · ble
nis/take′
nis′/tle/toe
mis/took′
mis/treat′/ment
mis′/tress
mis/trust′/ing · ly
mis′/un/der/stand′-
/ing
mis′/un/der/stood′
mis/us′/age
mi′ter
mit′i/gate
mit′i/ga′/tion
mix′/ture
mne/mon′ic
Mo′ab/ite
mo′bile
mo′bi/li/za′/tion
mo′bi/lize
moc′/ca/sin
mod′al (pert. to mode)
mod′el (pattern)
mod′/el/ing
mod′/er/ate
mod′/ern/ize
mod′/es · ty
mod′i/cum
mod′i/fi′/a · ble
mod′i/fi/ca′/tion
mod′i/fi′er
mod′i · fy
mod′i/fy′/ing
mo · diste′
mod′u/la′/tion
mo′dus o · pe/ran′di
mo′hair′
Mo · ham′/med
moi′e · ty (/ties)
mois′/ture
mo · las′/ses
mold′/a · ble
mold′ed
mo · lec′u/lar
mol′e/cule
mole′/hill′
mo′les/ta′/tion
mol′/li/fi/ca′/tion
mol′/lusk
Mol′o/tov
mo · lyb′/de/num

mo'men/tar'y
mo·men'/tous
Mon'a·co
mon'/ar/chy (/chies)
mon'/as/te'/ri·al
mon'/as/ter'y (/ies)
mo·nas'/tic
Mon'/day
mon'e/tar'y
mon'ey
mon'/ey/mak/ing
mon'/ger/ing
Mon/go'/lian
mon'/goose
mon'/grel
mon'i/ker
mo·ni'/tion
mon'i/tor
mon'/key/shine'
mon'/key wrench
monk'/ish
mon'o/chro/mat'ic
mon'o/chrome
mon'o/cle
mo·nog'a/mous
mon'o/graph
mon'o/lith
mon'o/logue
mon'o/me/tal'/lic
mon'o/plane
mo·nop'o/lize
mo·nop'o·ly (/lies)
mon'o/rail'
mon'o/syl'/la/ble
mon'o/tone
mo·not'o/nous
mon'o/type
mon/ox'/ide
mon'/sei/gneur'
mon/sieur'
(mes'/sieurs)
mon/si'/gnor
mon/soon'
mon'/ster
mon/stros'/i·ty (·ties)
Mon/tan'a
Mon'/te/zu'ma
Mont'/gom'/er·y
month'ly
Mont/pe'/lier, Vt.
mon'/tre·al'
mon'u/ment
mon'u/men'/tal
mood'i·ly
moon'/beam
moon'/light
moon'/struck
moor'/ish
mor'al (ethical)
mo·rale' (attitude)
mo·ral'/i·ty (·ties)
mo·rass'
mor'a/to'/ri·um
(/ri·a; /ums)

o·ra′/vi·an
or′/bid
or′/dant (caustic)
or′/dent
(musical embellishment)
ore/o′ver
orgue
or′i/bund
or′/mon (/mons)
orn′/ing
orn′/ing glo′ry
(/ries)
o·roc′co
o·rose′
or′/pheus
or′/phine
or′/sel
or′/tal
or/tal′/i·ty
or′/tar/board′
ort′·gage
ort′/ga/gee′
or/ti′/cian
or′/ti/fi/ca′/tion
or′/tise
or′/tu/ar′y (/ies)
o·sa′ic
os′/cow
o′ses
os′/lem
osque
os/qui′to (/toes)

moss′—/grown′
mo·tel′
moth′/er/hood
moth′er—/in—/law′
(moth′ers— . . .)
moth′/er/li/ness
mo·tif′
mo′tion/less
mo′ti/vate
mot′/ley
mo′tor/cy′/cle
mo′tor/ist
mot′/tle
mot′to (/toes)
mount′/a·ble
moun′/tain
moun′/tain/eer′
moun′/tain/ous
moun′/te/bank
mourn′/ing
mousse
mous/tache′
mouth′/piece′
mov′a/bil′/i·ty
mov′/a·ble
move′/ment
mov′ie
mov′/ing
mow′er
mu′ci/lage
mu′cous, *adj.*
mu′cus, *n.*

mud'/di/ness
mud'/dle
mud'dy
mud'/guard'
mud'/sling'er
muf'/fin
muf'/fler
mug'/wump'
muk'/luk
mu · lat'to (/toes)
mul'/ber'ry (/ries)
mulch (cover)
mulct (penalty)
mul'/li/gan
mul'/lion
mul'ti/far'i/ous
Mul'/ti/graph
mul'/ti/lat'/er · al
mul'/ti/mil/lion/aire'
mul'/ti/phase
mul'/ti/ple
mul'/ti/pli/cand'
mul'/ti/pli/ca'/tion
mul'/ti/plic'/i · ty
mul'/ti/pli'er
mul'/ti/tude
mul'/ti/tu'/di/nous
mum'my (/mies)
mun'/dane
mu · nic'i/pal
mu · nic'i/pal'/i · ty
(· ties)
mu'ni/ment
mu · ni'/tion
mu'ral
mur'/der
mu'rine
mur'/mur
mus'/ca/tel'
mus'/cle (tissue)
Mus'/co/vite
mus'/cu/lar
mu · se'um
mush'/room
mu'sic
mu'si/cal
mu'si/cale'
mu · si'/cian
Mus/ke'/gon, Mich.
mus'/ket/eer'
musk'/mel'on
musk'/rat
mus'/lin
mus'/sel (shellfish)
Mus'/so/li'ni
mus'/tache
mus'/tang
mus'/tard
mus'/ter
mus'/ti/ness
mu'ta/bil'/i · ty
mu'tate
mu'ti/late
mu'ti/nied

ı'ti · ny
ıt'/ter
ı'tu · al
u'tu/al · ly
uz'/zle
y · o'/pi · a
yr'i · ad
yrrh

myr'/tle
mys/te'/ri/ous
mys'/ter · y (/ies)
mys'/ti/cal
mys'/ti/cism
myth'/i · cal
my · thol'o · gy (/gies)
myth · o/log'/i · cal

N

a · celle'
a'dir
ai'ad
a · ive'
a · ïve · té'
a'ked
am'by—/pam'by
ame'/less
ame'ly
ame'/sake'
aph'/tha
ap'/kin
Ja · po'/le · on
ar/cis'/sus (/sus · es;
/cis'si)
ar/cot'ic
ar/ra'/tion
ar'/ra/tive
ar'row—/mind'ed

na'sal
nas'/cent
Nash'/ville, Tenn.
nas/tur'/tium
na'tal
Natch'ez
na'tion · al
na'tion/al/ism
na'tion/al'/i · ty (· ties)
na'tive
na · tiv'/i · ty (· ties)
nat'ty
nat'u/ral
nat'u/ral · i/za'/tion
nat'u/ral/ize
nat'u/ral · ly
nat'u/ral/ness
na'ture
naugh'/ti · ly

naugh'ty
nau'/se · a
nau'/seous
nau'/ti/cal
nau'/ti/lus (/lus · es;
/ti · li)
na'val (pert. to ships)
na'vel
(abdominal depression)
nav'i/ga/ble
nav'i/ga'/tion
Naz'a/rene'
Na'zism
Ne · an'/der/thal
Ne'a/pol'i/tan
near'by'
near'/sight'ed
near'sight'/ed · ly
neat'/ness
Ne · bras'ka
Neb'u/chad/nez'/zar
neb'u · la (/lae)
neb'u/lous
nec'/es/sar'i · ly
nec'/es/sar'y
ne · ces'/si/tate
ne · ces'/si · ty (/ties)
neck'/er/chief
neck'/ing
neck'/lace
neck'/tie
ne · crol'o · gy (/gies)
ne · crop'o/lis (/lis · es;
/les)
nec'/rop · sy
nec'/tar/ine'
née
need'/ful
need'i/ness
nee'/dle
nee'/dle/work
ne'er'—/do—/well'
ne · far'i/ous
ne · ga'/tion
neg'a/tive
neg'a/tiv/ism
ne · glect'
ne · glect'ed
neg'/li/gee'
neg'/li/gence
neg'/li/gi/ble
ne · go'/ti · a/bil'/i · ty
ne · go'/ti/a · ble
ne · go'/ti/ate
ne · go'/ti · a'/tion
Ne'gress
Ne'gro (groes)
neigh'/bor
neigh'/bor/hood
neigh'/bor/ing
nei'/ther
nem'a/tode
Nem'/bu/tal
nem'e/sis (/ses)

e'o/im/pres'/sion/ism
e'o/lith'ic
e'o/phyte
e'o/plasm
eph'ew
ep'o/tism
ep'/tune
erve'/less/ness
er'/vous
es'/tle
est'/ling
eth'/er/lands
eth'/er/most
et'/work'
eu/ral'/gia
eu'/ras/the'/ni·a
eu/ri'/tis
eu/ro'/gli·a
eu/rol'o·gy
eu'/ron
eu/ro'/sis (/ses)
eu/rot'ic
eu'/ter
eu/tral'/i·ty
eu'/tral·i/za'/tion
eu'/tron
Ie·vad'a
ev'/er/the/less'
Iew'/ark, N. J.
Iew'/found/land
Iew Guin'ea
Iew Hamp'/shire

New Ha'ven, Conn.
new'/born'
new'/com'er
new'/fan'/gled
New Jer'/sey
New Mex'i·co
New Or'le/ans, La.
New York
new'/ness
news'/boy'
news'/cast'er
news'/let'/ter
news'/mon'/ger
news'/pa'/per
news'/reel
news'/stand'
Ni·ag'a·ra
Nic'a/ra'/gua
nib'/ble
nib'/lick
ni'ce·ty (/ties)
niche
Nich'o/las
nick'el
nick'/el·o'/de·on
nick'/name
nic'o/tine
niece
nig'/gard·ly
night'/cap'
night'/dress'
night'/gown'

night'/hawk'
night'/in/gale
night'/long'
night'/mare'
night'/time'
ni'hil/ism
nim'/ble
nim'/bus (• bi;
/bus • es)
Nim'/itz
Nim'/rod
nin'/com/poop
nine'/pins
nine'/teen'
nine'/teenth'
nine'/ti/eth
nine'ty
nin'ny (/nies)
ninth
nip'/ple
Nip'/pon/ese'
ni' • sei'
ni'trate
ni'tro/gen
ni'tro/glyc'/er/ine
ni • trol'ic
ni'trous
nit'/wit'
no • bil'/i • ty (• ties)
no'ble/man (/men)
no'bod • y
noc/tur'/nal
noc'u/ous
nod'u/lar
nod'/ule
nog'/gin
noise'/less
noise'/mak'er
noi'/some
nois'i • ly
no • lo con/ten'/de • re
no • mad'ic
nom de plume
no'men/cla'/ture
nom'i/nal
nom'i/nated
nom'i/na'/tion
nom'i/nee'
non'/as/sess'/a • ble
non'/cha/lance
non'/com'
non/com'/ba/tant
non'/com/mis'/sioned
non'/com/mit'/tal
non com'/pos
men'/tis
non'/con/duc'/tor
non'/con/form'/ist
non'/de/script
non'/dis/tinc'/tive
non/en'/ti • ty (/ties)
none'/such
non/fea'/sance
non/fer'/rous

n/flam'/ma/ble
n'/in/flam'/ma/ble
n'/in/ter/ven'/tion
n'/me/tal'/lic
n'/pa/reil'
n'/par/tic'i/pat'/ing
n/par'/ti/san
n'/plus
n'/pro/duc'/tive
n/res'i/dent
n'/sense
n/sen'/si/cal
n'/stop'
n/un'/ion
o'/dle
on'/tide
or'/dic
or'/folk, Va.
or/mal'/i·ty (·ties)
orse'/man (/men)
orth Car'o/li'na
orth Da·ko'ta
orth'/east'
orth'/east'/er·ly
orth'/ern
or/we'/gian
ose'/bleed'
ose'/gay'
ose'/piece'
os/tal'/gi·a
os'/tra/da'/mus
os'/tril

nos'/trum
no'ta/bil'/i·ty (·ties)
no'ta/ble
no·tar'i·al
no'ta/rize
no'ta·ry (/ries)
no·ta'/tion
note'/book'
note pa'per
note'/wor'/thy
noth'/ing
no'tice
no'tice/a·ble
no'tic/ing
no'ti/fi/ca'/tion
no'ti/fied
no'ti/fy'/ing
no'tions
no'tion·al
no'to/ri'e·ty (/ties)
no·to'/ri/ous
no'—trump'
not'/with/stand'/ing
nou'/gat
nour'/ish/ment
nov'/el/ette'
nov'/el·ty (/ties)
No·vem'/ber
no·ve'na
nov'/ice
No'vo/cain
now'a/days'

no'where
nox'/ious
noz'/zle
nu'ance
nub'/bin
Nu'bi·an
nu'bi/lous
nu·cel'/lus (·li)
nu'cle·ar
nu'cle·us (cle·i)
nud'/ism
nu'di·ty (/ties)
nug'/get
nui'/sance
nul'/li/fi/ca'/tion
nul'/li·fy
num'/ber
numb'/skull'
nu'mer/a·ble
nu'mer/ate
nu'mer·a'/tion
nu'mer·a'/tor
nu·mer'/i·cal
nu'mer/ol'o·gy
nu'mer/ous
nu'mis/mat'/ics
nun'/cu/pa'/tive
nun'/ner·y (/ies)
nup'/tial
nurse'/maid'
nur'/ser·y (/ies)
nur'/ser·y/man (/men
nurs'/ling
nur'/ture
nut'/crack'er
nut'/hatch'
nut'/meg
nu'tri·a
nu'tri/ent
nu'tri/ment
nu·tri'/tion
nu·tri'/tious
nut'/shell'
nut'ty
nuz'zle
ny'lon
nymph
nym'/pho/ma'/ni·a

O

oars'/men
o·a'sis (·ses)
oat'/meal
ob'bli/ga'to (/tos)
ob'du/rate
o·be'/di/ence

·bei'/sance
b'e/lisk
·bese'
·be'/si·ty
·beyed'
·bit'u/ar'y (/ies)
ob·jec'/tion/a·ble
ob·jec'/tive
ob'jec/tiv'/ity
ob·jet d'art'
ob'li/ga'/tion
ob·lig'a/to'ry
o·bliged'
ob·lique'
ob·lit'/er/ate
ob·liv'i·on
ob·nox'/ious
ob·scene'
ob·scure'
ob·scu'/ri·ty (/ties)
ob'se/quy (/quies)
ob·ser'/vance
ob·ser'/vant
ob'ser/va'/tion
ob'so/les'/cence
ob'so/lete
ob'sta/cle
ob·stet'/ri/cal
ob·stet'/rics
ob'sti/na·cy (/cies)
ob'sti/nate
ob·strep'/er/ous
ob·struct'
ob·struc'/tion
ob·tain'/a·ble
ob·trude'
ob·tru'/sive
ob·tuse'
ob'vi/ate
ob'vi/ous
oc·ca'/sion
oc·ca'/sion/al·ly
oc'ci/den'/tal
oc·cip'i/tal
oc·clu'/sion
oc·cult'
oc'cu/pan·cy (/cies)
oc'cu/pa'/tion
oc'cu/pied
oc'cu·py
oc·curred'
oc·cur'/rence
oc·cur'/ring
o'ce/an'ic
o'cean/og'/ra/phy
o'·clock'
oc'ta/gon
oc·tag'o/nal
oc'tave
Oc·to'/ber
oc'to/ge/nar'i·an
oc'to/pus (/pus·es; ·top'o/des; ·to·pi)
oc'u/list

odd'/i·ty (·ties)
o'di/ous
o'dor/if'/er/ous
o'dor/ous
O·dys'/seus
od'ys/sey
Oed'i/pus
of'fal
off'/cast'
of·fend'er
of·fen'/sive
of'fered
of'fer/ing
of'fer/to'ry (/ries)
off'/hand'
of'fice boy
of'fice/hold'er
of'fi/cer
of·fi'/cial
of·fi'/ci/ate
of·fi'/cious
off'/ing
off'/ish
off'/set', *n.*
off'/set', *v.*
off'/shoot
off'/shore', *adj.*
off'/shore', *adv.*
off'/spring'
O·hi'o
of'ten
oil'cloth'
oil'/skin'
oil'y
oint'/ment
O'kla/ho'ma
old'—/fash'·ioned
old—/fo'gy·ish
old'/ster
old'—/tim'er
o'le/an/der
o'le·o/mar'/ga/rine
ol·fac'/to·ry
ol'i/garch'y (/ies)
ol'ive
O·lym'/pi·ad
O·lym'/pic
O'ma·ha, Neb.
om'e/let
om'i/cron
om'i/nous
o·mis'/sion
o·mit'
o·mit'/ted
om'ni/bus
om·nip'o/tent
om'ni/pres'/ent
om·nis'/cient
om·niv'o/rous
on'com'/ing
one—/half, *adj.*
one'/ness
on'er/ous
one'—/sid'ed

one'—/way', *adj.*
on'ion/skin'
on'look'er
on'rush'
on'set'
on'slaught'
on'ward
on'yx
o·pac'/i·ty (·ties)
o'pal/es'/cent
o·paque'
o'pen—/air', *adj.*
o'pen—/eyed'
o'pen/hand'ed
o'pen—/mind'ed
o'pen/ness
op'er·a
op'er/ated
op'er/at'ic
op'er·a'/tion
op'er·a/tive
op'er·a'/tor
op'er/et'ta
O·phe'/lia
o'pi/ate
o·pin'/ion
o·pin'/ion/at'ed
o'pi·um
o·pos'/sum
op·po'/nent
op'por/tune'
op'por/tu'/ni·ty
op·pos'/a·ble
op'po/site
op'po/si'/tion
op·pres'/sion
op·pres'/sive
op·pro'/bri/ous
op'ti/cal
op·ti'/cian
op'ti/mism
op'ti/mis'/tic
op'ti/mum
op'tion·al
op·tom'e/trist
op'u/lent
or'a·cle
or'ange/ade'
o·rang'u/tan'
or'a/tor'/i·cal
or'a/to'/ri·o (·os)
or'a/to'ry
or'bit
or'chard
or'ches/tra
or'chid
or·dain'
or·deal'
or'dered
or'der/li/ness
or'di/nance (law)
or'di/nar'i·ly
or'di/na'/tion
ord'/nance (munitions)

Or′e/gon
or′gan·dy (/dies)
or·gan′ic
or′ga/nism
or′ga/ni/za′/tion
or′ga/nized
or·gan′za
o′ri/en′/tal/ism
or′i/en/tate
o′ri/en/ta′/tion
or′i/fice
o·rig′i/nal
o·rig′i/nal′/i·ty
(·ties)
o·rig′i/nal·ly
o′ri/ole
O·ri′on
Or′lon
or′na/ment
or′na/men/ta′/tion
or·nate′
or′ner·y
or′ni/thol′o·gy
or′phan/age
Or′pheus
or′tho/don′/tist
or′tho/dox
or·thog′/ra/phy
(/phies)
or′tho/pe′/dic
os′cil/la′/tion
os′cil/la′/tor
os·cil′/lo/graph
os′cu/late
O·si′/ris
os·mo′/sis
os′si/fi/ca′/tion
os′si·fy
os·ten′/si/ble
os′ten/ta′/tious
os′te/ol′o·gy
os′te·o/path′ic
os′tra/cize
os′trich
oth′/er/wise′
Ot′ta·wa
ot′to/man (/mans)
our/selves′
out′/board′
out′/burst′
out′/doors′, *adv.*
out′/doors′, *n.*
out′/er/most
out′/go′/ing
out/land′/ish
out′/law′
out′/line′
out′/ly′/ing
out′/ma/neu′/ver
out′/put′
out/ra′/geous
out/stand′/ing
out/weigh′
o′va·ry (/ries)

o · va'/tion
o'ver/all'
o'ver/alls'
o'ver/bear'/ing
o'ver/charge', *v.*
o'ver/charge', *n.*
o'ver/draw'
o'ver/due'
o'ver/looked'
o'ver/rule'
o'ver/run'
o'ver/sight'
o'vert
o'ver/ture
o'ver/whelm'/ing
ow'ing
owned
own'/er/ship
Ox'ford
ox'i/da'/tion
ox'i/dize
ox'y/gen
oys'/ter
o'zone

P

pace'/mak'er
pach'y/derm
pa · cif'ic
pac'i/fist
pack'/age
Pa · de/rew'/ski
pad'/dle
pad'/lock'
pa'dre
Pa · du'/cah, Ky.
pa'gan/ism
pag'/eant · ry (/ries)
pa · go'da
pain'/less
pains'/tak'/ing
paint'/brush'
pa · ja'/mas
pal'/ace
pal'/at/a · ble
pal'/ate
(roof of mouth)
pa · la'/tial
pa · lav'er
pa'le/eth/nol'o · gy
pal'/ette (board for paint)
pal'i/sade'
pal/la'/di · um (/di · a)
pall'/bear'er
pal'/li · a'/tive
pal'/lor
palm'/is/try
pal'o/mi'no (/nos)

pal'/pa/ble
pal'/pi/ta'/tion
pal'sy
pam'/per
pam'/phlet
pan'a/ce'a
Pan'a · ma
Pan'—/A · mer'i · can
pan'/cake'
pan'/cre · as
pan'/de/mo'/ni · um
pan'e/gyr'ic
pan'/el/ing
pan'/el/ist
pan'/han'/dle
Pan'/hel/len'ic
pan'ic
pan'/icked
pan'/ick · y
pan'o/phy (/plies)
pan'o/ra'ma
pan'/ta/loon'
pan'/the · on
pan'/to/mime
pant'y/waist'
pa'pa · cy (/cies)
pa'pier—/mâ · ché'
pa · poose'
pa · pri'ka
pa · py'/rus (· py'ri)
par'/a · ble
pa · rab'o · la
par'a/chute
par'a/chut'/ist
pa · rade'
par'a/dise
par'a/dox'/i · cal
par'/af/fin
par'a/gon
par'a/graph
Par'a/guay
par'a/keet
par'/al/lel
par'/al/lel'o/gram
pa · ral'y/sis
par'a/lyzed
par'a/mount
par'a/pet
par'a/pher/na'/li · a
par'a/phrase
par'a/pleg'ic
par'a/site
par'a/sol
par'a/troop'er
par'/boil'
par'/cel
par'/cel post
par/chee'si
parch'/ment
par'/don/a · ble
par'e/gor'ic
par'/ent/age
pa · ren'/the/sis
(/the/ses)

pa·re'/sis
par/fait'
par·i/mu'/tu·el
pa·rish'/io/ner
Pa·ri'/sian
par'/i·ty
par'/lia/ment
par'/lia/men/tar'i·an
par'/lor
pa·ro'/chi·al
par'o·dy (/dies)
pa·rol' (oral)
pa·role' (a promise)
par'/ox/ysm
par/quet'
par/si/mo'/ni/ous
par'/son/age
Par'/the/non
par'/ti/al'/i·ty
par'/tial·ly
par/tic'i/pant
par/tic'i/pa'/tion
par'/ti/cip'i·al
par'/ti/ci/ple
par'/ti/cle
par/tic'u/lar·ly
par'/ti/san
par/ti'/tion
part'/ner/ship
par'/tridge
pass'/a·ble
pas'/sage
Pas/sa'ic, N. J.
pas·sé'
passed
pas'/sen/ger
pass/ers·by', *pl.*
pas'/sion/ate
pas'/sive
pass'/o'ver
pass'/port
paste
pas/tel'
Pas'/teur'
pas'/teur·i/za'/tion
pas'/time
pas'/to/ral
pas'/tor/ate
pas'/try
pas'/ture
pat'/ent/a·ble
pa·ter'/nal/ism
Pat'/er/son, N. J.
pa·thet'ic
path'/find'er
pa·thol'o·gy (/gies)
pa'thos
pa'tience
pa'tient
pa'ti·o (·os)
pa'tri/arch
pa·tri'/cian
pat'/ri/mo'ny
(/nies)

pa'tri/ot'ic
pa'tri·o/tism
pa·trol'
pa·trolled'
pa·trol'/ling
pa·trol'/man (/men)
pa'tron/age
pat'/tern
Pat'/ter/son, N. Y.
pau'/ci·ty
pau'/per
pause
pave'/ment
pa·vil'/ion
pawn'/bro'/ker
Paw/tuck'et, R. I.
pay'/a·ble
pay'ee'
pay'/roll
peace'/a·ble
pea'/cock
peal (sound)
pearl'y
peas'/ant·ry
pec'/ca/ble
pec'/ca/dil'lo (/loes)
pec'u/la'/tion
pe·cu'/li/ar'/i·ty
(·ties)
pe·cu'/ni/ar'y
ped'a/gog'/i·cal
ped'a/gogue
ped'/ant·ry (/ries)
ped'/dler
ped'/es/tal
pe·des'/tri·an
pe'di·a/tri'/cian
ped'i/cure
ped'i/gree
pe·dom'e/ter
peel (skin)
peer'/age
pee'/vish
Peg'a/sus
pei/gnoir'
Pe·king/ese'
pel'i/can
pe'nal·i/za'/tion
pen'/al·ty (/ties)
pen'/ance
pen'/chant
pen'/ciled
pen'/dant
pen'/den/cy
pen'/du/lum
pen'e/tra'/tion
pen'/guin
pen'i/cil'/lin
pen/in'/su·la
pen'i/tence
pen'i/ten'tia·ry
(/ries)
pen'/man/ship
pen'/nant

pen′/ni/less
Penn′/syl/va′/nian
pen′ny—/wise′
pe·nol′o/gist
pen′/sion·er
pen′/ta/gon
pen/tath′/lon
Pen′/te/cost
pent′/house′
pent/ste′/mon
pe·nu′/ri/ous
pe′on/age
pe′o·ny (/nies)
peo′/ple
pep′/per
pep′/per/mint
per/am′/bu/la′/tion
per an′num
per/cale′
per cap′i·ta
per/ceiv′/a·ble
per/cent′
per/cent′/age
per/cep′/ti/ble
per/cep′/tion
per/cep′/tu·al
per′/co/la′/tor
per/cus′/sion
per di′em
per/di′/tion
per′e/gri/na′/tion
pe·remp′/to·ry
pe·ren′/ni·al
per/fec′/tion
per′/fect·ly
per/fid′i/ous
per′/fi·dy (/dies)
per′/fo/rat′ed
per/for′/mance
per/fume′, *v.*
per′/fume, *n.*
per/func′/to·ry
per′/go·la
per/haps′
Per′i/cles′
per′/il/ous
pe·rim′e/ter
pe′ri/od′/i·cal
pe·riph′/er·y (/ies)
per′i/scope
per′/ish/a·ble
per′/ju·ry (/ries)
per′/ma/nent
per′/me·a/bil′/i·ty
per′/me/ate
per/mis′/si/ble
per/mis′/sion
per/mit′/ted
per′/mu/ta′/tion
per/ni′/cious
per′o/ra′/tion
per/ox′ide
per/pen/dic′u/lar
per′/pe/trate

per/pet'u·al
per/pet'u/ate
per'/pe/tu'/i·ty
(·ties)
per/plex'/ing
per/plex'/i·ty (·ties)
per'/qui/site
per se
per'/se/cu'/tion
Per'/seus
per'/se/ver'/ance
per'/se/vere'
Per'/sian
per'/si/flage
per/sim'/mon
per/sis'/tence
per'/son/a·ble
per'/son/al'/i·ty
(·ties)
per'/son/al·ly
per/son'i/fi/ca'/tion
per'son/nel'
per/spec'/tive, *n.*
per'/spi/ca'/cious
per'/spi/ra'/tion
per/spire'
per/suade'
per/sua'/sion
per/tain'
per'/ti/nent
per/turb'/a·ble
pe·rus'al
pe·ruse'
Pe·ru'/vi·an
per/vade'
per/ver'/sion
per/vert', *v.*
per'/vert, *n.*
per'/vi/ous
pes'/si/mism
pes'/si/mis'/tic
pes'/ti/cide
pes/tif'/er/ous
pes'/ti/lence
pe·ti'/tion
pe·ti'/tion/ar·y
pet'/ri/fi/ca'/tion
pe·tro'/le·um
pet'/ti/coat
pet'u/lant
pe·tu'/ni·a
pew'/ter
pfen'/nig
pha'e/ton
pha'/lanx
phan'/tom
phar'i/see
phar'/ma/ceu'/ti/cal
phar'/ma/cist
phar'/ma·cy (/cies)
phar'/ynx (/yn'/ges)
phase
pheas'/ant
phe'/no/bar'/bi/tal

phe/nom'e/non (·na)
Phil'a/del'/phi·a, Pa.
phi/lan'/der·er
phi/lan'/thro·py (/pies)
phi/lat'e·ly
phil'/har/mon'ic
Phil'/ip/pines, *but* Fil'i/pi'no
phi/los'o/pher
phi/los'o/phy (/phies)
phlegm
phleg/mat'ic
pho'/bi·a
Phoe/ni'/cian
Phoe'/nix, Ariz.
pho/net'ic
pho'/no/graph
phos'/phate
phos'/pho/rous, *adj.*
phos'/pho/rus, *n.*
pho'/to/en/grav'/ing
pho'/to/gen'ic
pho/tog'/ra/pher
pho'/to/gra/vure'
pho'to—/off'set
Pho'/to/stat, *n.*
phra'/se/ol'o·gy
phre/net'ic
phre/nol'o/gist
phys'/i·cal
phys'/i·cal·ly
phy/si'/cian
phys'/ics
phys'i/og'/no·my
phys'i/og'/ra/phy
phys'i/ol'o·gy
phy/sique'
pi'a/nis'/si·mo
pi·an'/ist
pi·an'o (·os)
pi·az'za
pi'ca
pic'a/yune'
Pic'/ca/dil'ly
pic'/co·lo (/los)
pick'/er·el
pick'et
pick'le
pick'/pock'et
pick'/up, *n., adj.*
pic'/nic
pic'/nick/ing
pic'/to/graph
pic/to'/ri·al
pic'/ture
pic'/tur/esque'
piece'/meal'
piece'/work'
pierc'/ing
pi'e·ty (/ties)
pi'geon/hole'
pig'/head'ed
pig'/men/ta'/tion

pig'/skin'
pil'/fer
pil'/grim/age
pil'/lage
pil'/lar
pil'/lo · ry (/ries)
pil'/low/case'
pi'lot/house'
pi · men'to (/tos)
pim'/ple
pin'a/fore'
pin'/cers
pin'/cush'/ion
pine'/ap'/ple
pin'/feath'er
Ping'—/Pong
pin'/head'
pin'/ion
pin'/na/cle
pi'noch'le
pin'/scher
pi'o/neer'
pi'ous
pipe'/line
pipe or'gan
pi'quan · cy
pique (irritation)
pi · qué' (corded fabric)
pi'ra · cy (/cies)
pir'/ou/ette'
pis'/ca/to' · ry
pis/ta'/chio (s)
pis'/til (plant ovary)
pis'/tol (gun)
pis'/ton
pit'—a—pat'
pitch'—/black'
pitch'er
pit'e/ous
pit'/fall'
pith'i/ness
pit'i/a · ble
pit'i/less
pit'/tance
pit'ter—/pat'ter
Pitts'/burg, Kan.
Pitts'/burgh, Pa.
pi · tu'i/tar'y
pit'y (/ies)
piv'/ot · al
piz'za
piz'/zi/ca'to
pla'/ca/bil'/i · ty
plac'/ard, *n.*
pla/card', *v.*
pla'/cate
place kick
place'/ment
pla/cen'ta
plac'/id · ly
plack'et
pla'/gi · a/rism
pla'/gi · a/rize
plague

plaid
plain'/ness
plain'/tiff, *n.*
plain'/tive, *adj.*
plait'/ing
plane
plan'et
plan'e/tar'i·um (·i·a)
planned
plan'/ning
plan/ta'/tion
plaque
plas'ma
plas'/ter·er
plas/tic'/i·ty
plat
plate
pla/teau'
plate glass
plat'en
plat'/form
plat'i/num
plat'i/tude
pla/ton'ic
pla/toon'
plat'/ter
plau'/dit
plau'/si/bil'/i·ty
play'/ground'
play'—/off'
play'/wright'
pla'za
plead'/a·ble
pleas'/ant·ry (/ries)
pleas'/ing
pleased
plea'/sur/a·ble
plea'/sure
pleat
ple/be'/ian
pleb'i/scite
pledg'ee'
Ple'/ia/des
plen'i/po/ten'/ti/ar'y (/ies)
plen'/te/ous
plen'/ti/ful
pleu'/ri·sy
plex'i/glass
pli'a/bil'/i·ty
pli'/ant
pli'/ers
plight
plot'/tage
plough
plow'/share'
plum'/age
plumb'er
plumb'/ing
plum'/met
plun'/der·er
plu/ral'/i·ty (·ties)
plu/toc'/ra·cy (/cies)
plu'/to/crat

ply'/wood'
pneu/mat'ic
pneu/mat'/ics
pneu/mo'/ni · a
pock'/et/book'
po'di · um (· di · a)
po'em
po'et · ry
poi'/gnan · cy
poi'/gnant
poin/set'/ti · a
point'—/blank', *adj., adv.*
point'/less
poise
poi'/son/ing
poi'/son/ous
po'ker
po'lar · i/za'/tion
pole'/cat
pole—vault, *v.*
po · lice'/man (/men)
pol'i · cy (/cies)
pol'i/cy/hold'er
pol'/ish
Pol'/ish
po · lite'/ness
po · lit'/i · cal
pol · i/ti'/cian
pol'i/tics
pol'ka
pol'/li/wog
poll tax
pol/lu'/tion
po'lo/naise'
pol'y/an'/dry
po · lyg'a · my
pol'y/glot
pol'y/gon
Pol'y/ne'/sian
pol'y/no'/mi · al
pol'y/syl/lab'ic
pol'y/tech'/nic
pom'/ace
po'made
pome'/gran'/ate
Pom'/er · a'/nian
pom'/mel
pom'/pa/dour
Pom/pe'/ian
pom'/pon
pom/pos'/i · ty
pomp'/ous
pon'/cho (/chos)
pon'/der/a · ble
pon'/der/ous
pon'/iard
pon'/tiff
pon/tif'/i · cal
pon/toon'
poor'/house
pop'/er · y
pop'/lin
pop'/py/cock'

pop'u/lar'/i·ty (·ties)
pop'u/la'/tion
pop'u/lous
por'/ce/lain
por'/cu/pine
por/nog'/ra/phy
po'rous
por'/poise
por'/ridge
por'/ta/ble
por/tend'
por'/tent
por/ten'/tous
por'/ter/age
por'/ter/house'
port/fo'/li·o (·os)
por'/ti·co (/coes)
por/tiere'
por'/tion
port'/li/ness
Port'/land
port/man'/teau
por'/trait
por'/trai/ture
por/tray'al
Por'/tu/guese
po·si'/tion
pos'i/tive·ly
pos'se
pos/sess'
pos/sessed'
pos/ses'/sion
pos/ses'/sive
pos/si/bil'/i·ty (·ties)
pos'/si/ble
pos'/si/bly
post'/age
post'al card
(P. O. card)
post card (view card)
post'/date'
post'/di/lu'/vi·an
post'er
pos/te'/ri·or
pos/ter'/i·ty
post/grad'u/ate
post'/hu/mous
post'/man (/men)
post'/mark
post'/mas/ter
post/mor'/tem
post of'fice
post'/paid'
post/pone'/ment
post'/script
pos'/tu/late
pos'/ture
po'ta/ble
po·tas'/si·um
po·ta'to (/toes)
pot'/bel'ly
po'ten·cy (/cies)
po'ten/tate
po·ten'/tial·ly

po'tion
pot'/pour/ri'
pot'/ter·y (/ies)
Pough/keep'/sie, N. Y.
poul'/tice
poul'/try
pound'/cake'
pound'—/fool'ish
pov'/er·ty
pow'/der·y
pow'/er/ful
pow'/wow'
prac'/ti/ca/ble
prac'/ti/cal
prac'/tice
prac'/tic/ing
prac/ti'/tion·er
prag'/ma/tism
Prague
prai'/rie
praise'/wor'/thy
prank'/ish
prayer book
preach'/ment
pre'/am'/ble
pre/ar/range'
pre/car'i/ous
pre/cau'/tion/ar'·y
pre/cede'
pre/ced'ed
pre'/ce/dence
pre/ce'/dent, *adj.*
prec'e/dent, *n.*
pre/cep'/tor
pre/ces'/sion·al
pre'/cinct
pre'/cious
prec'i/pice
pre/cip'i/tate
pre/cip'i/tous
pre/cise'
pre/ci'/sion
pre/clude'
pre/co'/cious
pre'/con/cep'/tion
pre/cur'/sive
pred'a/to'ry
pre'/de/ces'/sor
pre'/des/ti/na'/tion
pre'/de/ter'/mine
pre/dic'a/ment
pred'i/cate
pre/dict'/a·ble
pre'/di/lec'/tion
pre'/dis/po/si'/tion
pre/dom'i/nance
pre/dom'i/nant
pre/dom'i/na'/tion
pre—/em'i·nence
pre—/empt'
pre/fab'/ri/cate
pre'/fab/ri/ca'/tion
pref'/ace
pref'a/to'ry

pref'/er/a·ble
pref'/er/ence
pref'/er/en'/tial
pre/ferred'
pre/fer'/ring
pre/fix', *v.*
pre'/fix, *n.*
preg'/nan·cy (/cies)
pre'/his/tor'ic
prej'u/dice
prej'u/di'/cial
prel'/ate
pre/lim'i/nar'y (/ies)
pre'/lude
pre'/ma/ture'
pre/med'/i·cal
pre'/med·i/ta'/tion
pre'/mi·er (chief)
pre/miere'
(first performance)
prem'/ise, *n.*
pre'/mi·um
pre'/mo/ni'/tion
pre/na'/tal
pre/oc'/cu/pa'/tion
pre/paid'
prep'a/ra'/tion
pre/pa'/ra/to'ry
pre/pare'
pre/par'/ed/ness
pre/pay'/ment
pre/pon'/der/ance
prep'o/si'/tion
pre'/pos/ses'/sion
pre/pos'/ter/ous
pre/req'/ui/site
pre/rog'a/tive
pres'/age, *n.*
pre/sage', *v.*
Pres'/by/te'/ri·an
pres'/by/ter'y (/ies)
pre'/sci/ent
pre/scribe'
pre/scrip'/tion
pres'/ence
pres'/ent, *adj.*
pre/sent', *v.*
pre'/sen/ta'/tion
pre/sen'/ti/ment
pres'/ent·ly
pre/sent'/ment
pres'/er/va'/tion
pre/serve'
pre/side'
pres'i/den·cy (/cies)
pres'i/dent
pres'i/den'/tial
pre/si'/di·o (·os)
pres'/sure
pres'/ti/dig'i/ta'/tor
pres/tige'
pre/sume'
pre/sump'/tion
pre/sump'/tu/ous

pre'/tense
pre/ten'/sion
pre/ten'/tious
pre'/text
pret'/ti·ly
pret'/zel
pre/vail'
prev'a/lence
pre/var'i/cate
pre/vent'/a·ble
pre/ven'/tive
pre'/vi/ous
pre'/vi/ous·ly
price'/less
pride'/ful
priest'/hood
pri'/ma·cy (/cies)
pri'ma don'na
pri'ma fa'ci·e
pri/mar'i·ly
pri'ma·ry (/ries)
prime'ly
prim'er
pri/me'/val
prim'i/tive
pri'/mo/gen'i/ture
pri/mor'/di·al
prim'/rose
prince'ly
prin'/cess
prin'/ci/pal
(*See* p. 233)
prin'/ci/pal'/i·ty
(·ties)
prin'/ci/pal·ly
prin'/ci/ple
(*See* p. 233)
prin'/ter
pri'or
pri/or'/i·ty (·ties)
prism
pris/mat'ic
pris'on
pris'/on·er
pris'/tine
pri'/va·cy (/cies)
pri'/vate
pri'/va/teer'
pri/va'/tion
priv'i/lege
priv'i·ty (·ties)
priv'y (/ies)
prize fight
prob'a/bil'/i·ty (·ties)
prob'/a·ble
prob'a/bly
pro'/bate
pro/ba'/tion/ary
prob'/lem
prob'/lem/at'/i·cal
pro/bos'/cis
pro/ce'/dure
pro/ceed', *v.*
pro'/ceed, *n.*

pro/ceed'ed
pro/ceed'/ings
pro'/cess
pro/ces'/sion · al
pro/claimed'
proc'/la/ma'/tion
pro/cliv'/i · ty
pro/cras'/ti/nate
pro'/cre · a'/tion
proc'/tor
proc/to'/ri · al
proc'u/ra/tor
pro/cured'
prod'i/gal
pro/di'/gious
prod'i · gy (/gies)
pro/duce', *v.*
pro'/duce, *n.*
pro/duc'er
prod'/uct
pro/duc'/tion
pro'/duc/tiv'/i · ty
prof'a/na'/tion
pro/fane'
pro/fan'/i · ty (/ties)
pro/fes'/sion · al
pro/fes'sor
pro'/fes/so'/ri · al
prof'/fer
pro/fi'/cien · cy (/cies)
pro/fi'/cient
pro'/file
prof'/it/a · ble
prof'i/teer'
prof'/li/ga · cy
prof'/lu/ent
pro/fun'/di · ty (/ties)
pro/fuse'
pro/fu'/sion
pro/gen'i/tor
prog'e · ny (/nies)
prog/no'/sis (/ses)
prog/nos'/ti/ca'/tion
pro'/gram
prog'/ress, *n.*
pro/gress', *v.*
pro/gres'/sive
pro/hib'it
pro'/hi/bi'/tion
pro/hib'i/tive
pro/ject', *v.*
proj'/ect, *n.*
pro/jec'/tile
pro/jec'/tion
pro'/le/tar'i · at
pro/lif'ic
pro'/logue
pro'/lon/ga'/tion
prom'e/nade'
Pro/me'/theus
prom'i/nence
pro/mis'/cu/ous
prom'/ise
prom'/is/so'ry

prom'/on/to'ry (/ries)
pro/mot'er
pro/mo'/tion
prompt'ly
prompt'/ness
pro'/mul/gate
pro'/noun
pro/nounce'/a·ble
pro/nun'/ci·a'/tion
proof'/read'er
proofs
pro'/pa/gan'da
prop'a/ga'/tion
pro/pone'
pro/pel'
pro/pel'/lant
pro/pelled'
pro/pen'/si·ty (/ties)
prop'/er·ly
prop'/er·ty (/ties)
proph'e·cy, *n.* (/cies)
proph'e·sy, *v.*
pro/phet'ic
pro'/phy/lac'/tic
pro/pin'/qui·ty
pro/pi'/tious
pro/por'/tion/ate
pro/pos'al
pro/pose'
prop'o/si'/tion
pro/pound'
pro/pri'e/tar'y
pro/pri'e/tor
pro/pri'e/tor/ship'
pro/pri'e·ty (/ties)
pro/pul'/sion
pro ra'ta
pro/rat'/a·ble
pro/sa'ic
pro/scribe'
pros'e/cute
pros'e/cu'/tor
pros'e/lyte
pros'/pect
pro/spec'/tive, *adj.*
pro/spec'/tus
pros/per'/i·ty (/ties)
pros'/per/ous
pros'/tate
pros'/ti/tute
pros'/ti/tu'/tion
pros/tra'/tion
pro/tag'o/nist
pro/tec'/tion
pro/tec'/tor/ate
pro'/té·gé
pro'/tein
pro tem'/po·re
pro/test', *v.*
pro'/test, *n.*
prot'/es/tant
Prot'/es/tant/ism
pro'/to/col
pro'/to/plasm

ro'/to/type
ro'/to/zo'on (/zo'a)
ro/trac'/tion
ro/trude'
ro/tru'/sion
ro/tu'/ber/ance
rov'/a·ble
rov'en
rov'/erb
ro/ver'/bi·al
ro/vid'ed
rov'i/dence
rov'i/den'/tial
rov'/ince
ro/vin'/cial
ro/vi'/sions
ro/vi'so (/sos)
rov·o/ca'/tion
ro/voc'a/tive
pro/vok'/ing
pro'/vost
prow'/ess
prox/im'/i·ty
prox'i·mo
prox'y (/ies)
pru'/dence
prud'/ish
Prus'/sian
psalm'/ist
pseu'/do/nym
psy/chi'a/try
psy'/cho/a·nal'y/sis
psy'/cho/log'/i·cal
psy/chol'o·gy
psy/chom'e/try
psy'/cho/path'ic
psy/cho'/sis (/ses)
pto'/maine
pu'ber·ty
pub'/lic
pub'/li/ca'/tion
pub/lic'/i·ty
pub'/lic u·til'/i·ties
pub'/lish·er
pud/ding
pueb'lo (/los)
pu'er/ile
Puer'to Ri'co
pu'gil/ist
pug/na'/cious
pu'is/sance
pul'/chri/tude
pul'/chri/tu'/di/nous
pul'ley
Pull'/man
pul'/mo/nar'y
pul'/mo'/tor
pul'/pit
pul'/sate
pul/sa'/tion
pul'/ver/ize
pum'/ice
pum'/per/nick'el
pump'/kin

punc/til'i/ous
punc'/tu·al
punc'/tu/al'/i·ty (·ties)
punc'/tu/ate
punc'/tu·a'/tion
punc'/ture
pun'/gen·cy
pun'/ish/a·ble
pun'/ish/ment
pu'ni/tive
pun'/ster
pu'pil
pup'/pet·ry
pur'/chas/a·ble
pur'/chas/ing
pure'/ness
pur'/ga/tive
pur'/ga/to'ry
purge
pu'ri/fi/ca'/tion
pur'/ist
pu'ri/tan'/i·cal
Pu'ri/tan/ism
pu'ri·ty (/ties)
pur/loin'
pur'/plish
pur/port', *v.*
pur'/port, *n.*
pur'/pose
pur'/pos/ive
purs'er
pur/su'/ant
pur/sue'
pur/su'/ing
pur/suit'
pur/ver'/ance
puss'y/foot'
pu'tre/fac'/tion
pu'tre·fy
pu'trid
put'/ting
puz'/zle
puz'/zling
Pyg/ma'/li·on
pyg'my (/mies)
pyk'/nic (stocky)
py'or/rhe'a
pyr'a/mid
py·ram'i/dal
pyre
py'thon

Q

quack'/er·y (/ies)
quad'/ran'/gle
quad'/ri/lat'/er·al
qua/dril'/lion
qua/droon'
qua/dru'/ple
qua/dru'/pli/cate
quaff
quag'/mire
quaint
Quak'er
qual'i/fi/ca'/tion
qual'i/fied
qual'i/fy'/ing
qual'i/ta'tive
qual'/i·ty (·ties)
qualm
quan'/da·ry (/ries)
quan'/ti/ta'/tive
quan'/ti·ty (/ties)
quan'/tum (·ta)
quar'/an/tine
quar'/reled
quar'/rel/ing
quar'/rel/some
quar'ry
quar'/ter
quar'/ter/back'
quar'/ter·ly
quar'/ter/mas'/ter
quar/tet'
quartz
quash
qua'si
quay
queen
queer
quell
quench'/less
quer'u/lous
que'ry (/ries)
ques'/tion/a·ble
ques'/tion/naire'
quib'/ble
quick'/lime'
quick'ly
quick'/sand'
quick'—/wit'ted
qui/es'/cence
qui'et
qui'e/tude
qui·e'/tus
quill
quilt'/ing

qui'/nine
quin/tes'/sence
quin/tet'
quin'/tu/plet
quire
quirk
quit'/claim'
quite
quit'/tance
quiv'er
quix/ot'ic
quiz (quiz'/zes)
quizzed
quiz'/zi/cal
quiz'/zing
quo'/rum
quot'/a · ble
quo/ta'/tion
quot'ed
quo'/tient

R

rab'bi
rab'/bit · ry (/ries)
rab'/ble
ra'bid
ra'bies
rac/coon'
race'/course'
ra'cial
Ra · cine', Wis.
rack'e/teer'
rac'/on/teur'
ra'dar
ra'di · al
ra'di/ance
ra'di · a'/tion
ra'di · a'/tor
rad'i/cal/ism
ra'di · o (· os)
ra'di · o/ac/tiv'/i · ty
ra'di · o/gram
ra'di · o/te/leg'/ra/phy
rad'/ish
ra'di · um
ra'di · us (· di · i)
raf'/fle
raft'er
rag'a/muf'/fin
rag'/ged
ra · gout'
rag'/time'
rag'/weed'
rail'/road'
rail'/way'
rai'/ment

in'/bow'
in check
in'/coat'
in wa'ter
i'/sin
i/son d'être'
'ja
k'/ish
a'leigh
l'ly (/lies)
m'/bling
m'i/fi/ca'/tion
m'—/jet en'gine
m/page'
m'/pant
m'/part
m'/rod'
m'/shack'le
anch'er
an'/cid
an'/cor/ous
an'/dom
ange
an'/kle
an'/sack
an'/som
a·pa'/cious
Ra'pha·el
a·pid'/i·ty
a'pi·er
rap'/ine
rap/port'

rap/scal'/lion
rap'/tur/ous
rar'e/fac'/tion
rar'e·fy
rar'/i·ty (·ties)
ras/cal'/i·ty (·ties)
rasp'/ber'ry (/ries)
ratch'et
rate'a/bil'/i·ty
rath'er
raths'/kel'/ler
rat'i/fi/ca'/tion
rat'i/fy'/ing
rat'/ing
ra'tio (·tios)
ra·ti·o/ci/na'/tion
ra'tion·al
ra'tion/al/ize
rat/tan'
rat'/tle/brained'
rat'/tle/snake'
rat'/tle/trap'
rau'/cous
rav'/age
rav'/en/ous
rav'/ish
raw'/boned'
raw'/hide'
ray'on
ra'zor/back'
re·ac'/tion/ar'y (/ies)
read'/a·ble

read'i/ness
re'ad/just'/ment
re'ad/mis'/sion
read'y
read'y—/made'
read'y—/to—/wear'
re'af/firm'
re·a'/gent
re'al es·tate', *n.*
re'al—/es·tate', *adj.*
re'al/ism
re'al·i/za'/tion
re'al·ly
realm
re'al/tor
re'al·ty
ream
re·an'i/mate
reap'er
re'ap/pear'/ance
re'ap/point'
rear guard
rea'/son/a·ble
re'as/sem'/ble
re'as/sign'/ment
re'as/sur'/ance
re'·bate
re·bel', *v.*
reb'el, *adj., n.*
re·bel'/lion
re·bel'/lious
re·birth'
re·bound'
re·buff'
re·buke'
re·but'/tal
re·cal'/ci/trant
re·call'
re·cant'
re'ca/pit'u/la'/tion
re·cap'/ture
re·cede'
re·ceipt'
re·ceipt'ed
re·ceiv'/a·ble
re·ceived'
re·ceiv'/er/ship
re·ceiv'/ing
re'cent·ly
re·cep'/ta/cle
re·cep'/tion
re·cess'
re·ces'/sion·al
rec'i·pe
re·cip'i/ent
re·cip'/ro/cal
re·cip'/ro/cate
rec'i/proc'/i·ty
re·cit'al
rec'i/ta'/tion
re·cite'
reck'/less
reck'/on/ing
re·claim'

c'/la/ma'/tion
·cline'
·cluse'
c'/og/ni'/tion
·cog'/ni/zance
c'/og/nize
·coil'
c'/ol/lect' (to recall)
'—/col·lect'
(collect again)
ec'/ol/lec'/tion
ec'/om/mend'
ec'/om/men/da'/tion
ec'/om/mend'ed
ec'/om/pense
ec'/on/cile
ec'/on/cil'i/a'tion
e·con'/nais/sance
e'con/noi'/ter
e·con'/quer
e'con/sid'er
e'con/struc'/tion
ec'/ord, *n.*
re·cord', *v.*
re·coup'
re·course'
re·cov'/er·y (/ies)
rec'/re·a'/tion
re·crim'i/na'/tion
re·cruit'
rec'/tan/gle
rec'/ti/fi'er
rec'/ti·fy
rec'/ti/tude
re·cum'/bent
re·cu'/per/ate
re·cur'
re·curred'
re·cur'/rence
red'/dish
re·deem'
re·deem'/a·ble
re·demp'/tion
re'dis/trib'/ute
re·dress'
re·duce'
re·duc'/i·ble
re·duc'/tion
re·dun'/dance
reef'er
re·e/lect'
re·e/lec'/tion
re·en'/ter
ref'/er·ee'
ref'/er/ence
ref'/er/en'/dum
(/dums; /en'da)
re·ferred'
re·fer'/ring
re·fine'/ment
re·fin'/er·y (/ies)
re·flec'/tion
re·flec'/tor
re'flex

re′flo/res′/cence
re•for′/est
re′for/es/ta′/tion
ref′/or/ma′/tion
re•for′/ma/to•ry
re•formed′
re•frac′/to•ry
re•frain′
re•fresh′/ment
re•frig′/er/ate
re•frig′/er•a′/tion
ref′/uge
ref′u/gee′
re•fund′
re•fur′/bish
re•fus′al
ref′u/ta′/tion
re•ga′/li•a
re•gard′/less
re•gat′ta
re′gen•cy (/cies)
re•gen′/er/ate
re•gen′/er•a/tor
re′gent
re•gime′
reg′i/ment
reg′i/men/ta′/tion
re′gion•al
reg′/is/ter
reg′/is/tered
reg′/is/trant
reg′/is/tra′/tion
re•gres′/sion
re•gret′
re•gret′/ta/ble
re•gret′/ted
reg′u/lar•ly
reg′u/la′/tion
re•gur′/gi/tate
re′ha/bil′i/tate
re′ha/bil′i/ta′/tion
re•hears′al
re•hearse′
reign (rule)
re′im/burse′
re′im/pose′
rein (to check)
re′in/car′/nate
rein′/deer′, *sing. & pl.*
re′in/flate′
re′in/forced′
re′in/sert′
re′in/state′
re•it′/er/ate
re•ject′
re•joice′
re•join′/der
re•ju′/ve/nate
re•kin′/dle
re•lapse′
re•lat′ed
re•la′/tion
rel′a/tive
re′lax•a′/tion

'/layed
·lease'
·leased'
l'e/gate
·lent'/less
l'e/vant
·li'a/bil'/i·ty
·li'/ance
l'ic
·lief'
·lieve'
·li'/gion
·lin'/quish
el'/ish
e·lo'/cate
e·luc'/tance
e·ly'
e·main'/der
e·mand'
em'a/nent, *adj.*
e·mark'/a·ble
e·mar'ry
Rem'/brandt
e·me'/di·al
em'e·dy (/dies)
e·mem'/ber
e·mem'/brance
e·mind'er
em'i/nis'/cence
e·miss'
e·mis'/sion
e·mit'

re·mit'/tance
re·mit'/ted
rem'/nant
re·mod'el
re·mod'/eled
re·mon'/strance
re·mon'/strate
re·morse'
re·mote'
re·mov'/a·ble
re·mov'al
re·mu'/ner·a'/tion
re·mu'/ner·a'/tive
re·nais/sance'
ren/coun'/ter
ren'/der
ren'/dez/vous
ren/di'/tion
ren'e/gade
re·nege'
re·new'al
re·nom'i/nate
re·nounce'
ren'o/vate
ren'o/va'/tion
re·nowned'
rent'al
re·num'/ber
re·nun'/ci·a'/tion
re·or'/der
re·or/ga/ni/za'/tion
re·pair'

rep'a/ra'/tion
rep'/ar/tee'
re·pa'/tri/ate
re·pay'/ment
re·peal'
re·peat'ed
re·peat'/ed·ly
re·pel'/lent
re·pen'/tance
re'per/cus'/sion
rep'/er/toire
rep'e/ti'/tion
re·phrase'
re·place'/ment
re·plen'/ish
re·plen'/ish/ment
re·plete'
re·plev'in
rep'/li·ca
re·ply' (·plies')
re·port'er
re·pos'i/to'ry (/ries)
re'·pos/sess'
rep'/re/hen'/si/ble
rep'/re/sent'
rep'/re/sen/ta'/tion
rep/re/sen'/ta/tive
re·pres'/sion
re·prieve'
rep'/ri/mand
re'print
re·pris'al
re·proach'/ful
rep'/ro/bate
re·pro/duce'
re'pro/duc'/tion
re·proof'
re·prove'
rep'/tile
re·pub'/lic
re·pub'/li/can
re·pu'/di/ate
re·pugn'
re·pug'/nance
re·pulse'
re·pul'/sion
rep'u/ta/ble
rep'u/ta'/tion
re·quest'
re'qui·em
re·quire'/ment
req'/ui/site
req'/ui/si'/tion
re·quite'
re·sal'/a·ble
re·scind'
res'/cue
re·seal'
re·search'
re/sem'/blance
re·sent'/ment
res'/er/va'/tion
re·serve'
re·served'

s'/er/voir
s'i/dence
s·i/den'/tial
·sid'u·al
s'i/due
·sid'u·um (·u·a)
s/ig/na'/tion
·signed'
·sil'/ience
·sil'/ien·cy
s'/in/ous
·sis'/tance
·sis'/tor
s·o/lu'/tion
·solve'
·sol'/vent
s'o/nance
·sort'
·sound'
'source
·spect·a/bil'/i·ty
s/pi/ra'/tion
'spi/ra/to·ry
s'/pite
·splen'/dence
·spon'/dent
·sponse'
·spon/si/bil'/i·ty
(·ties)
e·spon'/sive
e·state'
es'/tau/rant
res/ti/tu'/tion
res'/tive
rest'/less
res/to/ra'/tion
re·store'
re·straint'
re·stric'/tion
re·sul'/tant
re·sume'
ré'su·mé
re·sump'/tion
re·sur'/gence
res/ur/rec'/tion
re·sur/vey'
re·sus'/ci/tate
re·sus/ci/ta'/tion
re'tail
re·tain'er
re·tal'i/ate
re·tal·i/a'tion
re·tar/da'/tion
re·ten'/tion
ret'i/cent
ret'i·na
ret'i/nue
re·tire'/ment
re·tort'
re·tract'
re·trac'/tion
re·trench'/ment
re·treat'
ret/ri/bu'/tion

re·trieve'
re'tro/ac'/tion
re'tro/ces'/sion
ret'/ro/grade
re'tro/gres'/sion
re'tro/spect
re·turn'/a·ble
re·un'/ion
re'u·nite'
re·val'u/ate
re·veal'
rev'/eil·le
rev'e/la'/tion
rev'/el·er
re·venge'
re·venge'/ful·ly
rev'e/nue
re·ver'/ber·a'/tion
re·vere'
rev'/er/ence
rev'/er/end
re·ver'/sal
re·vers'/i·ble
re·ver'/sion
re·view'er
re·vise'
re·vi'/sion
re·vi'/tal/ize
re·viv'al
rev'o/ca/ble
rev'o/ca'/tion
re·volt'/ing
rev'o/lu'/tion/ar'y
rev'o/lu'/tion/ize
re·volv'er
re·vue'
re·vul'/sion
re·ward'
rhap'/so·dy (/dies)
rhet'o/ric
rhe/tor'/i·cal
rheu/mat'ic
rheu'/ma/tism
rhine'/stone'
rhi/noc'/er·os
rhi'/zoid
Rhode Is'land
rho'/do/den'/dron
rhom'/boid
rhom'/bus (/bus·es; rhom'bi)
rhon'/chus (/chi)
rhu'/barb
rhythm
rhyth'/mic
rhyth'/mi/cal
rib'/bon
Ri'che/lieu'
rich'/est
rick'/rack'
ric'o/chet'
rid'/dance
ridge
rid'i/cule

·dic'u/lous
d'/ing
ff'/raff'
'fle/man (/men)
g'a/doon'
g'/ger
ght'/eous
ght'/eous/ness
ght'—/hand'ed
ght of way
ig'id
i·gid'/i·ty
ig'/ma/role
ig'/or/ous
ing'er
ing'/lead'er
ing'/side'
inse
Ri'o de Ja·nei'ro
i'ot/ous
ip'/cord'
ip'/ple
ip'—/roar'ing
is'/ing
is/qué'
it'u·al
i'val
i'valed
i'val/ing
i'val·ry (/ries)
iv'/er/side
iv'et

riv'u/let
road'/bed'
road'/house'
road'/ster
road'/way'
roar'/ing
rob'/ber·y (/ies)
ro'bot
ro·bust'
Ro·chelle'
Roch'/es/ter, N. Y.
rock—/bot'tom, *adj.*
rock'et
rock'/ing chair
ro'dent
ro'de·o (·os)
roent'/gen
ro'guish
role (player's part)
roll
rol'/lick/ing
ro'ly—/po'ly
ro'maine
Ro'man/esque'
Ro·ma'/nian
ro·man'/tic
ro·man'/ti/cism
Ro'me·o
room/ette'
room'/mate'
Roo'/se/velt
roost'er

Roque'/fort
ro'sa·ry (/ries)
rose'—/col'ored
ros'/ter
ros'/trum (/tra; /trums)
Ro·tar'i·an
ro'ta·ry
ro·ta'/tion
ro'tis'/se/rie'
ro'to/gra/vure'
rot'/ten
ro·tun'da
rouge
rough'/age
rough'/house'
rough'/neck'
rough'/shod'
rou/lette'
round'/a·bout'
round'ed
round'/house'
round'—/shoul'dered
round'up'
rous'/ing
roust'/a·bout'
rou/tine'
row'/boat'
row'/dy/ish
roy'/al/ist
roy'alty
Ru·bái'yát'
rub'/ber/ize
rub'/ber/neck'
rub'/bish
rub'/ble
rub'/down'
Ru'bi/con
ruck'/sack
rud'/der
ru'di/ment
rue'/ful·ly
ruf'/fi·an
ruf'/fle
rug'/ged
ru'in/ous
rum'/ble
ru'mi/nate
rum'/mage
ru'mor
rum'/pus
run'a/bout'
run'/a·way'
run'/down
run'—/in'
run'/ner
run'ner—up'
run'/ning
run'/way'
rup'/ture
ru'ral
rus'/set
Rus'/sian
rus'/tic

rus/tic'/i·ty (·ties)
rus'/tle
ru'ta/ba'ga
ruth'/less

S

Sab'/bath
sab/bat'/i·cal
sa'ber—/toothed'
sa'ble
sab'o/tage'
sac'/cha/rin
sac'/er/do'/tal
sa'chem
sa·chet'
sack'/cloth'
sac'/ra/ment
Sac'/ra/men'to, Calif.
sa'cred
sac'/ri/fice
sac'/ri/fi'/cial
sac'/ri/le'/gious
sac'/ris/tan
sac'/ro/sanct
sa'crum (sa'cra)
sad'/dest
sad'/dle
sad'/i'ron
sad'/ness
sa·fa'ri
safe—/de·pos'it box
safe'/guard
safe'/keep'/ing
safe'ly
safe'ty
saf'/flow'er
saf'/fron
sa·ga'/cious
sa·gac'/i·ty (·ties)
sage'/brush'
Sag'/it/ta'/ri·us
sa·gua'ro (/ros)
sail'/cloth'
sail'or
St. Lou'is, Mo.
St. Paul, Minn.
sal'/a·ble
sa·la'/cious
sal'ad
sal'a/man'/der
sa·la'mi
sal'a·ry (/ried, /ries)
sales'/man (/men)
sales'/wom'an
(/wom'en)
sa'lient

sa'line
sa·li'va
salm'on, *sing. & pl.*
sa·lon'
sa·loon'
sa·lu'/bri/ous
sal'u/tar'y
sal'u/ta'/tion
sa·lute'
sal'/vage
sal/va'/tion
salve
Sa·mar'i/tan
Sa·mo'a
sam'o/var
sam'/ple
sam'/pling
San An·to'/ni·o, Tex.
san'a/to'/ri·um (/ri·a)
sanc'/ti/mo'/ni/ous
sanc'/tion
sanc'/ti·ty (/ties)
sanc'/tu/ar'y (/ies)
sanc'/tum
san'/dal
san'/dal/wood'
San Di·e'go, Calif.
sand'/wich
San'/for/ized
San Fran/cis'co
san'/guine
san·i/tar'/i·an
san·i/tar'i·um (/ums; ·i·a)
san'i/tar'y
san'i/ta'/tion
San Jo·se', Calif.
San Juan
San'/skrit
San'ta Fe, N. Mex.
San'/ti·a'go
sa·pon'i·fy
sap'/phire
sa·ran'
sar'/casm
sar/cas'/tic
sar/co'ma (/ma·ta; /mas)
sar'/dine
sar/don'ic
sa·rong'
sar/to'/ri·al
Sas/katch'e/wan
sas'/sa/fras
sa·tan'ic
satch'el
sa·teen'
sat'/el/lite
sa'ti/ate
sat'·in
sat'/ire
sat'/is/fac'/tion
sat'/is/fac'/to/ri·ly

sat'/is/fac'/to·ry
sat'/is·fy (fied)
sat'u/rate
Sat'/ur/day
Sat'/urn
sauce
sau'/cer
sau'cy
sauer'/kraut'
Sault Sainte Marie
sau'na
saun'/ter
sau'/sage
sau·té'
sau/terne'
sav'/age
Sa·van'/nah
sa·vant'
sav'/ing
sa'vor·y
saw'/dust
saw'—/toothed'
sax'o/phone
says
scab'/bard
sca'/brous
scaf'/fold
scal'a/wag
sca/lene'
scal'/lion
scal'/loped
scal'/pel
scam'/per
scan'/dal
Scan'/di/na'/vi·an
scant'i/ness
scape'/goat'
scarce'ly
scar'/ci·ty
scare'/crow'
scarf (scarves)
scar'/let
scarred
scath'/ing
scat'/ter
scat'/ter/brain'
scav'/en/ger
sce/nar'i·o (·os)
scen'/er·y
sce'/nic
scent
scep'/ter
sched'/ule
sched'/uled
sche/mat'ic
scheme
Sche/nec'/ta·dy, N. Y.
schil'/ling
schip'/per·ke
schism
schiz'o/phren'ic
schnau'/zer
schol'/ar/ship
scho/las'/tic

school'/house
schoon'er
sci/at'i·ca
sci'/ence
sci'/en/tif'/i·cal·ly
sci'/en/tist
scim'i/tar
scin'/til/late
sci'on
scis'/sors
scle/ro'/sis (/ses)
scoffed
scoot'er
scorch
scorn'/ful
scor'/pi·on
scot'—/free'
scoun'/drel
scour'/ing
scourged
scout'/ing
scout'/mas'/ter
scram'/ble
scrap'/book'
scrape
scrap'/ple
scratch'y
scrawl
scream'/ing
screech
screen'/ing
screw'/ball'
scrib'/ble
scrim'/mage
script
scrip'/ture
scro'/tum (·ta)
scroung'er
scrubbed
scrump'/tious
scru'/ples
scru'/pu/lous
scru'/ti/nize
scru'/ti·ny (/nies)
scuf'/fle
scul'/ler·y (/ies)
scul'/lion
sculp'/tor
sculp'/ture
scum'my
scur'/ril/ous
scur'ry
scut'/tle
scythe
Sea'/bee'
sea'/far'/ing
seal'/ing wax
seal'/skin'
sea'/man/ship
seam'/stress
sé'ance'
sea'/plane'
searched
search'/light'

sea'/shore'
sea'/sick'/ness
sea'/son·al
sea'/son/a·ble
Se·at'/tle, Wash.
se·ba'/ceous
se'cant
se·cede'
se·ces'/sion
se·clude'
se·clu'/sion
sec'/on/dar·y
sec'/ond/hand', *adj.*
se'cre·cy
se'cret
sec'/re/tar'i·al
sec'/re/tar'y (/ies)
se·cre'/tion
sec/tar'i·an
sec'/tion
sec'/tion/al·ly
sec'/tor
sec'u/lar
se·cure'
se·cur'/ing
se·cu'/ri·ty (/ties)
se·dan'
se·date'
sed'a/tive
sed'/en/tar'y
sed'i/ment
se·di'/tion
se·di'/tious
se·duce'/ment
se·duc'/tion
sed'u/lous
se'dum
seed'/ling
see'/ing
seem'/ing·ly
seem'ly
seep'/age
seer'/suck'er
see'/saw'
seethe
seg'/ment
seg'/re/gate
seg'/re/ga'/tion
seine
seis'/mo/graph
seis/mol'o/gist
seiz'/a·ble
seized
sei'/zure
sel'/dom
se·lec'/tion
se·lec'/tiv'/i·ty
se·le'/ni·um
self'—/cen'tered
self'—/con'fi·dence
self'—/con·trol'
self'—/ex·plan'a·to'ry
self'/ish
self'—/made'

self'—/sac'ri·fice
self'—/start'er
sell'er
sell'/out'
sel'/vage
se·man'/tics
sem'a/phore
sem'/blance
se'men (sem'i·na)
se·mes'/ter
sem'i/an'/nual
sem'i/cir'/cle
sem'i/co'/lon
sem'i/fi'/nal/ist
sem'i/month'ly
sem'i/nar'y (/ies)
sen'/ate
sen'a/tor
sen'a/to'/ri·al
se'nile
se·nil'/i·ty
se·nior'/i·ty
sen/sa'/tion·al
sense'/less
sen'/si/bil'/i·ty (·ties)
sen'/si/tiv'/i·ty (·ties)
sen'/si/tize
sen'/so·ry
sen'/su·al
sen'/su/ous
sen'/tence
sen/ten'/tious
sen'/tient
sen'/ti/ment
sen'/ti/men'/tal
sen'/ti/nel
sen'/try (/tries)
sep'a/ra/ble
sep'a/rate·ly
sep'a/ra'/tion
se'pi·a (·as; se'pi·ae)
Sep/tem'/ber
sep/ten'/ni·al
sep'/tic
sep'/tu/plet
sep'/ul/cher
se·qua'/cious
se'quel
se·quen'/tial
se·ques'/ter
se'quin
se·quoi'a
se·ra'pe
se·raph'ic
ser'e/nade'
se·rene'
se·ren'/i·ty (·ties)
serge
ser'/geant
ser'/geant at arms
se'ri·al
se'ri/ous·ly
ser'/mon/ize
ser'/pen/tine

ser'/rate
se'rum (·rums; ·ra)
ser'/vant
served
ser'/vice
ser'/vice/a·ble
ser'/vile
ser/vil'/i·ty
ser'/vi/tude
ser'/vo/mech'a/nism
ses'a·me
ses'/qui/cen/ten'/ni·al
ses'/sion
set'/back'
set/tee'
set'/ter
set'/tle/ment
set'/tler
set'—to' (—/tos')
set'up'
sev'/en/teen'
sev'/er·al
sev'/er/ance
se·ver'/i·ty (·ties)
sew'/age
sew'/er/age
sex'a/ge/nar'i·an
sex/en'/ni·al
sex'/tant
sex'/ton
sex/tu'/plet
sex'u·al
sex'u/al'/i·ty
shab'/bi/ness
shack'le
shad'ow
shake'/down'
Shake'/speare
shal'/low
sham'/ble
shame'/faced'
sham/poo' (/poos')
Shang'/hai
Shan'gri—La'
shape'/less
share'/crop'/per
share'/hold'er
sharp'/en·er
sharp'—/eyed'
sharp'/shoot'er
shav'er
shear (cut)
sheathe
sheep'/herd'er
sheep'/ish
sheep'/skin'
sheer (thin)
sheet'/ing
shek'el
shel/lac'
shel/lacked'
shel'/ter
shelv'/ing
shep'/herd

Sher'a/ton
sher'/bet
sher'/iff
sher'ry
shield
shift'/less
shil'/ling
shim'/mer
shin'/gles
shin'/ing
Shin'/to/ism
ship'/board'
ship'/build'er
shipped
ship'/shape'
ship'/wreck'
shirt'/waist'
shiv'er
shock'/ing
shod'dy
shoe'/horn'
shoe'/ing
shone
shoot'/ing
shop'/keep'er
shop'/lift'er
shop'/worn'
short'/age'
short'/cake'
short'/en/ing
short'/hand'
short'—/lived'
short'/sight'ed
short'/stop'
shoul'/der
should'n't
shov'el
shov'/eled
show'/case'
show'er bath
show'i·ly
show'/room'
shrap'/nel
shred'/ded
shrewd
shriek
Shrin'er
shrink'/age
shriv'/eled
shroud'/less
shrub'/ber·y (/ies)
shrunk'en
shuf'/fle
shuf'/fle/board'
shut'/down'
shut'—in', *n., adj.*
shut'/ter
shut'/tle/cock'
Shy'/lock
shy'/ster
Si·a/mese'
sib'i/lant
Si·cil'/ian
sick'en

sick'/en/ing
sick'le
sick'ness
side'/board'
side'/sad'/dle
side'/walk'
side'/ways'
siege
si·er'ra
Sieg'/fried
si·es'ta
sieve
sight'/less
sight'—/see'ing
sig'/naled
sig'/na/to'ry
sig'/na/ture
signed
sig'/net
sig/nif'i/cance (/ant)
sig'/ni/fied
sign'/post'
si'lage
si'lence
si'lex (quartz silica)
sil'/hou/ette'
sil'i/con
silk'i/ness
silk'/worm'
sil'/li/ness
si'lo (·los)
sil'/ver/smith'
sil'/ver/ware'
sim'i·an
sim'i/lar'/i·ty (·ties)
sim'i·le
si·mil'i/tude
sim'/mer
sim'/ple
sim'/ple/ton
sim/plic'/i·ty (·ties)
sim'/ply
sim'u/late
si'mul/ta'/ne/ous
sin/cere'
sin/cer'/i·ty
si'ne/cure
si'ne' di'e
sin'/ew·y
sin'/ful
singe'/ing
sing'er
sin'/gle/hand'ed
sin'gle—/mind'ed
sin'/gle/ton
sing'/song'
sin'/gu/lar
sin'/is/ter
sink'/age
sin'/ner
sin'u/ous
si'nus
Sioux City, Iowa
si'phon

si'ren
sir'/loin'
sis'ter—/in—/law'
(sis'ters— . . .)
sit'/ting
sit'u/at'·ed
sit'u/a'tion
six'/teen'
six'/ti/eth
siz'/a·ble
siz'/zle
skat'/ing
skein
skel'e/ton
skep'/ti/cal
sketch'/book'
skew'er
ski'/ing
skil'/let
skill'/ful
skim'/ming
skimp'y
skin'/flint'
skin'ny
skip'/per
skir'/mish
skit'/tish
skiv'/vies
skul/dug'/ger·y
skulk
skull'/cap'
sky'/cap
sky'/light'
sky'/rock'et
sky'/scrap'er
slack'er
sla'/lom
slain
slan'/der/ous
slant'/ing
slashed
slat'/tern
slaugh'/ter
slav'/er·y
slea'zy
sled'/ding
sleep'/less
sleeve
sleigh
sleight
slen'/der/ize
sleuth
slick'er
slid'/ing
slight'ly
sling'/shot'
slip'/o'ver, *adj., n.*
slipped
slip'/per·y
slip'/shod'
slith'er
sliv'er
slob'/ber
slo'/gan

sloth'/ful
slouch
slough
slov'/en · ly
slug'/gard
sluice
slum'/ber
small'/pox'
smash' up
smat'/ter/ing
smell'/ing
smith'/er/eens'
smoke'/less
smold'er
smooth'/bore'
smooth'er
smor'/gas/bord
smoth'er
smudge
smug'/gle
smut'ty
snaf'/fle
snap'/drag'on
snap'/per
snap'/pish/ness
snare'/drum
snarl'/ing
snatch
sneak'er
sneer'/ing
sneeze
snick'er
snif'/fle
sniv'el
snob'/ber · y
snoop'y
snor'/kel
snow'/storm'
snub'—/nosed'
snuf'/fle
snug'/gle
soap'/box'
soap'i/ness
soap'/suds'
sob'er—/mind'ed
so · bri'e · ty
so'bri/quet
sob sis'/ter
so'—/called'
soc'/cer
so'cia/ble
so'cial/ism
so'cial/ite
so · ci'e · ty (/ties)
so'ci/ol'o · gy
sock'et
Soc'/ra/tes
sod'/den
so'di · um
sof'/ten
soft'/heart'ed
soi/ree'
so · journ'
so'lace

so·lar'i·um (·i·a)
sol'/der
sol'/dier
sol'e/cism
sol'/emn
so/lem'/ni·ty (/ties)
sol'/em/nize
so'le/noid
so·lic'it
so·lic'i/ta'/tion
so·lic'i/tous
sol'i/dar'/i·ty (·ties)
so·lid'i·fy
so·lil'o/quize
so·lil'o/quy (/quies)
sol'i/taire
sol'i/tar'y
sol'i/tude
so'lo (·los)
Sol'o/mon
sol'u/ble
so·lu'/tion
solv'/a·ble
sol'/ven·cy (/cies)
sol'/vent
som'/ber
som/bre'ro (/ros)
some'/bod'y
some'/one'
som'/er/sault
some'/thing
some'/times'
som'/no/lent
so·na'ta
song'/stress
son'—/in—/law'
(sons'— . . .)
son'/net
so·no'/rous
soon'er
soothe
sooth'/say'er
so·phis'/ti/cat'ed
so·phis'/ti/ca'/tion
soph'/ist·ry (/ries)
soph'o/more
so'po/rif'ic
so·pran'o (·os)
Sor/bonne'
sor'/cer·er
sor'/did
sor'/ghum
so·rop'/ti/mist
so·ror'/i·ty (·ties)
sor'/rel
sor'/row/ful
SOS
souf'/flé'
sought
soul'/less
sound'/ing
sound'/proof
source
sou'/sa/phone

South Car'o/lin'a
South Da·ko'ta
South'/er/ner
south'/west'
sou'/ve/nir'
sov'/er/eign
sov'/er/eign·ty (/ties)
so'vi·et
spa'/cious/ness
spa/ghet'ti
span'/gle
span'/iel
Span'/ish
spank'/ing
spar'/ing·ly
spar'/kle
spar'/kling
spar'/row
Spar'/tan
spasm
spas/mod'ic
spas'/tic
spat'/ter
spat'u·la
speak'—/eas'y
speak'/ing
spear'/mint'
spe'/cial
spe'/cial/ize
spe'/cial·ly
spe'/cial·ty (/ties)
spe'/cie
spec'i/fi/ca'/tion
spe/cif'ic
spec'i·fy
spec'i/men
spe/cious
spec'/ta/cle
spec/tac'u/lar
spec/ta'/tor
spec'/tral
spec'/tro/scope
spec'/trum (/tra)
spec'u/late
spec'u/la'/tion
speech'/less
speed'i·ly
speed/om'e/ter
spell'/bound'
spell'/ing
Spen/ce'/ri·an
spend'/thrift'
spher'/i·cal
sphinx
spic'i/ness
spick'—/and—/span'
spi'/der
spig'ot
spill'/way'
spin'/ach
spi'/nal
spin'/dle
spine'/less
spin'/ster

spi'/ral
spir'/it•ed
spir'/it•u/al/ism
spir'/it•u/al'/i•ty
  (•ties)
spite'/ful
spit'/fire
splat'/ter
splen'/did
splin'/ter
split'/ting
splurge
splut'/ter
spoil'/age
spo'/li•a'/tion
Spo/kane', Wash.
spokes'/man (/men)
spong'/ing
spon'gy
spon'/sor
spon'/ta/ne'/i•ty
  (•ties)
spon/ta'/ne/ous
spook'/ish
spoon'/ful (/fuls)
spo/rad'ic
sports'/man/ship
sports'/wear'
spot'/light'
spot'/ted
sprain
spread
spring'/board'
Spring'/field
spring'/time'
sprin'/kle
sprock'et
sprout
spruce
spu'/ri/ous
spurn
Sput'/nik
sput'/ter
spu'/tum (•ta)
spy'/glass'
squab'/ble
squad'/ron
squal'id
squall
squal'or
squan'/der
square
squash'/ing
squat'/ter
squaw
squawk
squeak
squeak'i/ness
squeam'/ish
squee'/gee
squeeze
squelch'er
squir'/rel
sta/bil'/i•ty

sta'/ble
stac/ca'to (/tos)
sta'/di·um (/ums)
stage'/coach'
stage'/craft'
stag'/ger
stag'/nant
stag/na'/tion
staid
stain'/less
stair'/case'
stake'/hold'er
sta/lac'/tite
sta/lag'/mite
stale'/mate'
stal'/lion
stal'/wart
sta'/men
stam'i·na
stam'/mer
stam/pede'
stanch
stan'/dard
stan'/dard/ize
stand'by, *n., adj.*
stand'point'
stan'za
sta'/ple
star'/board
starch'i/ness
stare
star'/fish'
star'/let
star'/light'
starred
star'/tle
star'/tling
star/va'/tion
state'/craft'
state'/ment
states'/man (/men)
stat'ic
stat'/ing
sta'/tion/ar'y (fixed)
sta'/tion·er
sta'/tion/er'y (paper)
sta'/tis'/ti/cal
stat'/is/ti'/cian
sta/tis'/tics
stat'u/ar'y (/ies)
stat'u/esque
stat'u/ette'
stat'/ure
sta'/tus
sta'/tus quo
stat'/ute
stat'u/to'ry
stayed
stead'/fast
stead'i·ly
stealth'i·ly
steal (pilfer)
steam'/ship
steel (commercial iron)

stee'/ple/chase'
steer'/age
sten'/cil
ste/nog'/ra/pher
ste/nog'/ra/phy
sten·o/graph'ic
step'/child'
(/chil'/dren)
step'/lad'/der
stepped
ste'/re·o
ste/re·o/pho'/nic
ste'/re·o/type
ster'/ile
ste/ril'i·ty
ster'i/lize
ster'/ling
steth'o/scope
ste'/ve/dore'
stew'/ard/ess
stick'i/ness
stick'—/to'—/it·ive
·ness
stiff'en
stig'ma
stim'u/lant
stim'u/lus (·li)
stin'/gi/ness
sti'/pend
stip'u/late
stip'u/la'/tion
stir'/rup
stitch
stock/ade'
stock'/bro'/ker
stock'/hold'er
stock'/ings
stock'/yard'
sto'ic
stol'id
stom'/ach
stone'/cut'/ter
stooge
stop'/gap'
stop'/page
stopped
stor'/age
store'/keep'er
store'/room'
sto'ry (/ries)
stout'/ness
stow'/a·way'
strag'/gle
straight
straight'/ened
strain
strait
strait'—/laced'
strange
strange'ly
stran'/gle
stran'/gu/late
strap'/ping
strat'a/gem

stra/te'/gic
strat'e·gy (/gies)
strat'o/sphere
stra'/tum (stra'ta)
straw'/ber'ry (/ries)
streak'y
stream'er
stream'/lined'
street'/car'
strength'en
stren'u/ous
strep'/to/coc'/cus (/coc'ci)
strep'/to/my'/cin
stressed
stretched
strick'en
strict'ly
stric'/ture
stri'/dent
strik'er
strik'/ing·ly
strin'/gen·cy
striped
strol'/ler
stron'/ger
struc'/tur·al
strug'/gle
strut'/ting
strych'/nine
stub'/ble
stub'/born·ly
stub'/born/ness
stuc'co (/coes)
stud'/ding
stu'/dent
stud'/ied
stu'/di·o (·os)
stu'/di/ous
stud'y/ing
stuff'i/ness
stul'/ti·fy
stum'/ble
stun'/ning
stu/pen'/dous
stu'/pid/i·ty (·ties)
stu'/por
stur'/di/ness
stur'/dy
stut'/ter·er
styl'/ish
sty'/lus
sty'/mie
sty'/rene
sty'/ro/foam
suave
sub'/com/mit'/tee
sub/con'/scious
sub/con'/tract
sub'/di/vi'/sion
sub/due'
sub'/ject, *adj., n.*
sub/ject', *v.*
sub/jec'/tive

sub'/ju/gate
sub/junc'/tive
sub'/lease'
sub'/li/mate
sub/lim'i/nal
sub/ma/rine'
sub/merge'
sub/mis'/sion
sub/mit'/ted
sub/nor'/mal
sub/or'/di/nate
sub/or'/di/na'/tion
sub/poe'na
sub'/ro/gate
sub/ro'sa
sub/scribe'
sub/scrib'er
sub/scrip'/tion
sub'/se/quent
sub/ser'/vi/ent
sub/side'
sub/sid'i/ar'·y (/ies)
sub'/si/dize
sub'/si·dy (/dies)
sub/sis'/tence
sub'/soil
sub'/stance
sub/stan'/dard
sub/stan'/tial
sub/stan'/ti/ate
sub'/sti/tute
sub/sti/tu'/tion
sub'/ter/fuge
sub'/ter/ra'/ne·an
sub'/tile
sub'/ti'/tle
sub'tle
sub/trac'/tion
sub'/tra/hend'
sub'/urb
sub/ur'/ban
sub/ur'/ban/ite
sub/ver'/sion
sub'/way'
suc/ceed'
suc/cess'/ful
suc/ces'/sion
suc/ces'/sor
suc/cinct'
suc'/cor
suc'/co/tash
suc'/cu/lent
suc/cumb'
suck'er
suck'/ling
suc'/tion
sud'/den·ly
suede
su'et
suf'/fer/a·ble
suf'/fered
suf/fice'
suf/fi'/cient
suf'/fix, *n.*

ıf'/fo/cate
uf'/frage
ug'/ar/cane
ug/gest'ed
ug/ges'/tion
ug/ges'/tive
u'i/cide
u'ing
uit'/a·ble
uite (series; set)
uit'or
u'ki/ya'ki
ul'/fate
ul'/fur
ulk'i/ness
ul'/len
ul'/tan
ul'/try
um'/ma/ri·ly
um'/ma/rize
um'/ma·ry (/ries)
um/ma'/tion
um'/mer
um'/mit
um'/mons
ump'/tu/ous
Sun'/day
un'/dries
unk'en
un'/shine'
u'per/an'/nu/ate
su·perb'

su'per/charge'
su'per/cil'·i/ous
su'per/fi'/cial
su'per/hu'/man
su·per'/flu/ous
su'per/im/pose'
su·per/in/ten'/dent
su·pe'/ri·or
su'pe/ri/or'i·ty
su·per'/la/tive
su·per/mar'/ket
su'per/sede'
su'per/son'ic
su'per/sti'/tion
su'per/sti'/tious
su'per/vise'
su·per/vi'/sion
su'pine
sup/plant'
sup'/ple/ment
sup'/ple/men'/ta·ry
sup'/pli/cant
sup/ply' (/plies')
sup/port'
sup/pose'
sup'/po/si'/tion
sup/press'
su·prem'a·cy
su·preme'
sur/cease', *v.*
sure'ly
sure'ty (/ties)

sur'/faced
sur'/feit
surged
sur'/geon
sur'/ger·y
sur'/gi/cal
sur/mise'
sur/mount'ed
sur'/name'
sur/pass'
sur'/plice (a robe)
sur'/plus
sur/pris'ed
sur/pris'/ing·ly
sur/re'/al/ism
sur/ren'/der
sur'/rep/ti'/tious
sur'/ro/gate
sur/round'
sur/tax'
sur/veil'/lance
sur'/vey, *n.*
sur/vey', *v.*
sur/vey'or
sur/viv'al
sur/vi'/vor
sus/cep'/ti/ble
sus'/pect, *n.*
sus/pect', *v.*, *adj.*
sus/pend'er
sus/pense'
sus/pen'/sion
sus/pi'/cion
sus/pi'/cious
sus/tained'
sus'/te/nance
su'ture
swag'/ger
swal'low—/tailed'
swarth'y
swas'/ti·ka
swathed
sweat'ed
sweat'er
Swed'/ish
sweet'/heart'
swel'/ter
swerve
swim'/mer
swin'/dler
switch'/board'
swiv'el
syc'a/more
syc'o/phant
syl/lab'ic
syl'/la/ble
syl'/la/bus (/bus·es; /la·bi)
sylph
syl'/van
sym'/bol
sym/bol'ic
sym/met'/ri/cal
sym'/me/try

ym'/pa/thet'ic
ym'/pa/thize
ym'/pa/thy (/thies)
ym'/pho · ny (/nies)
ym/po'/si · um (/si · a;
 /ums)
ymp'/tom
yn'a/gogue
yn'/chro/nize
yn/co/pa'/tion
yn'/co · pe
yn'/di/cate
yn/ec'/do/che
yn'od

syn'o/nym
syn/on'y/mous
syn/op'/sis (/ses)
syn'/tax
syn/thet'ic
syn'/the/sis (/ses)
syn'/the/size
Syr'a/cuse, N. Y.
sy · ringe'
syr'up
sys'/tem
sys'/tem/at'ic
sys'/tem · a/tize
sys'/to · le

ab'/er/na/cle
ab'/leau (/leaux)
a'ble d'hôte'
a'ble/spoon/ful'
 (/fuls)
ab'/let
ab'/loid
a · boo' (· boos')
ab'u/late
a · chis'/to/scope'
a · chom'e/ter
ac'it
ac'i/turn

tack'le
Ta · co'ma, Wash.
tact'/ful
tac'/ti/cal
taf'/fe · ta
Ta · hi'/tian
tai'/lor
tai'lor–/made'
Taj Ma · hal'
take'–/home, *adj.*
take'/off, *n.*
tak'/ing
tal'/cum

tal'/ent·ed
tales'/man (/men) (juryman)
tal'/is/man (/mans) (a charm)
talk'a/tive
Tal'/la/has'/see, Fla.
tal'/low
tal'on
ta·ma'le
tam'a/rack
tam'/bou/rine'
tamp'er, *n.* (one who tamps)
tam'/per, *v.* (meddle)
tam'/pon
tan'/dem
tan'/gent
tan'/ge/rine'
tan'/gi/ble
tan'/gled
tan'go (/gos)
tan'/nic
tan'/ta/lize
tan'/ta/mount'
tan'/trum
ta'pered
tap'/es/try (/tries)
tap'/room'
tare (weight of container)
tar'/get
tar'/iff
tar'/nished
tar/pau'/lin
tar/tar'ic
task'/mas'/ter
tas'/seled
taste'/less
tat'/ting
tat/too' (/toos')
taught
taunt
taut
tav'/ern
taw'/dry
tax·a'/tion
tax'i/cab
tax'i/der'my
teach'/a·ble
teach'er
team'/ster
tear (rip; eye drop)
tease
tea'/spoon/ful' (/fuls)
tech'/ni/cal
tech/ni'/cian
Tech'/ni/col'or
tech/nique'
te'di/ous
Tel/Au'/to/graph
tel'e/gram
tel'e/graph
te·leg'/ra/pher
te·lep'a/thy

ɪl′e/phone
ɪl′e/scope
'el′e/type
ɪl′e/vise
ɪl′e/vi′/sion
ɪll′er
ɪll′/tale′
e·mer′/i·ty
em′/per·a/ment
em′/per/ance
em′/per/ate
em′/per·a/ture
em/pes′/tu/ous
em′/plate
em′/ple
em′/po/rar′y
em′/po/rize
emp/ta′/tion
en′/a·ble
e·na′/cious
e·nac′i·ty
en′/ant
en′/den·cy (/cies)
en′der
en′/don
en′e/ment
Ten/nes/see′
en′/nis
en′on
en′/sile
en′/sion
en′/ta/cle
ten′/ta/tive
ten′u/ous
ten′/ure
te·quil′la
ter′/mi/nal
ter′/mi/nate
ter′/mi/nol′o·gy
ter′/mite
ter′/race
ter/rain′
Ter′re Haute, Ind.
ter/res′/tri·al
ter′/ri/ble
ter′/ri·er
ter′/ri·fy
ter′/ri/to′/ri·al
ter′/ri/to′ry (/ries)
ter′/ror/ism
tes′/ta/ment
tes/ta′/tor
tes′/ti·fy
tes′/ti/mo′/ni·al
tes′/ti/mo′ny (/nies)
tet′a/nus
tête′—/à—/tête′
Teu/ton′ic
Tex′as
text′/book′
tex′/tile
tex′/ture
Thack′/er·ay
Thames

thanks/giv'/ing
the'a/ter
the/at'/ri/cal
theme
them/selves'
thence
the'o/log'/i·cal
the/ol'o·gy (/gies)
the'o/rem
the'o/ret'/i·cal
the'o/rize
the'o·ry (/ries)
ther'a/peu'/tics
ther'a·py
there/aft'er
there/for' (for it)
there'/fore (hence)
ther'/mal
ther'/mo/dy/nam'/ics
ther/mom'e/ter
ther'/mo/stat
the/sau'/rus
the'/sis (/ses)
they're (they are)
thief (thieves)
thigh
thim'/ble
think'/ing
thin'/ner
thirst'y
thir'/teen'
this'/tle

thith'er
tho/rac'ic
tho'/rax
thor'/ough/fare'
thor'/ough·ly
though
thought'/ful
thou'/sand
thread'/bare'
threat'en
three'/some
thresh'er
thresh'/old
thrift'i/ness
thrill'/ing·ly
thriv'/ing
throat'y
throe (a pain)
throm/bo'/sis
throne (seat)
throng
throt'/tle
through/out'
thrown (pitched)
thumb'/tack'
thun'/der
Thurs'/day
thwart
thy'/roid
tick'et
tick'le
tid'al

tier (row; layer)
ti'ger
tight'en
til'/ing
till'/a·ble
tim'/ber/land'
time'/keep'er
time'/ta'/ble
ti·mid'/i·ty
tim'/ing
tim'·o/rous
tinc'/ture
tin'/der
tinge'/ing
tin'/gled
tin'/ker
tip'/toe'
ti'rade
tired
tire'/some
tis'/sue
tithe
ti'tle
tit'u/lar
toast'/mas'/ter
to·bac'co (/cos)
to·bac'/co/nist
to·bog'/gan
to·day'
toe'/ing
tof'/fee
to·geth'er
tog'/gle
toi'/let
toil'/some
To'ky·o
To·le'do, Ohio
tol'/er/a·ble
tol'/er/ance
tol'/er·a'/tion
toll'/gate'
tom'a/hawk
to·ma'to (/toes)
tomb'/stone'
tom'/cat'
tom'/fool'/er·y (/ies)
to·mor'/row
to·nal'/i·ty (/ties)
tongs
tongue
to·night'
ton'/nage
ton/neau' (/neaus)
ton'/sil/lec'/to·my
ton'/sil/li'/tis
ton/so'/ri·al
ton'/tine
too (also; more than enough)
tooth'/ache'
tooth'/brush
to'paz
To·pe'ka, Kan.
top'/i·cal

to·pog'/raph·er
top' se'cret
top'sy—/tur'vy
tor'e/a·dor'
tor/ment', *v.*
tor'/ment, *n.*
tor/na'do (/does)
tor/pe'do (/does)
tor'/por
torque
tor/ren'/tial
tor'/rid
tor'/sion
tor'so (/sos)
tor/til'la
tor'/tu/ous
tor'/ture
toss'up'
to·tal'i/tar'i·an
to·tal'/i·ty
to'tal·ly
to'tem
touch'/down'
tough'en
tou/pee'
tour'/ist
tour'/na/ment
tour'/ney
tour'/ni/quet
to'wards
towns'/folk'
towns'/peo'/ple
town'/ship
tox·e'/mi·a
trace'/a·ble
tra'/che·a
tra/cho'ma
trac'/ing
track'/less
trac'/ta/ble
trade'—in'
trade'/mark
trade name
tra/di'/tion
tra/duce'
traf'/fic (*See* p. 228)
tra/ge'/di/enne', *fem.*
trag'e·dy (/dies)
trail'er
trai'/tor/ous
tra/jec'/to·ry (/ries)
tram/po/line
tran/quil'/li·ty
trans/act'
trans/ac'/tion
trans/ceiv'er
tran/scen'/dent
tran/scribe'
tran/scrip'/tion
trans/fer', *v.*
trans'/fer, *n.*
trans/fer'/a·ble
trans/fer'/ring
trans/fig'u/ra'/tion

rans/fix′
rans′/for/ma′/tion
rans/form′er
rans/gres′/sor
ran′/sient
ran/sis′/tor
ran′/si/tive
rans/la′/tion
rans/lu′/cent
trans/mi′/grate
trans/mis′/sion
trans/mit′/ted
trans′/mu/ta′/tion
tran′/som
trans/par′/ency
trans/plant′
trans′/por/ta′/tion
trans′/po/si′/tion
trans/ship′
tran′/sub/stan′/ti · a′-
/tion
trans/verse′
tra/peze′
trap′e/zoid
trau′ma (/ma · ta)
tra/vail′
trav′/eled
trav′/el · er
trav′/el/ing
tra/verse′, *v.*
trav′/es · ty (/ties)
treach′/er/ous
treach′/er · y (/ies)
tread
trea′/son
trea′/sure
trea′/sur · er
trea′/sur · y
trea′/tise
treat′/ment
trea′ty (/ties)
tre′/ble
trem′/ble
tre/men′/dous
trem′or
Tren′/ton, N. J.
trep′i/da′/tion
tres′/pass · er
tres′/tle
tri′ad
tri′al
tri′/an/gle
trib′u/la′/tion
tri/bu′/nal
tri′/bune
trib′u/tar′y (/ies)
trib′/ute
trick′/er · y (/ies)
tri′/cy/cle
tri/en′/ni · al
tri′/fle
trig′/ger
trig′o/nom′e · try
tril′o · gy

tri/mes'/ter
trimmed
trim'/ming
trin'/ket
tri/par'/tite
tri'/ple
trip'/li/cate
tri'/pod
trip'/ping
tri'/umph
tri/um'/vi/rate
triv'i·al
trol'/ley
trom'/bone
troop (group of people)
tro'/phy (/phies)
trop'ic
trou'/ba/dour
trou'/ble/some
trough
troupe (traveling actors)
trou'/sers
trous'/seau (/seaux')
trout
trow'el
tru'/an·cy
tru'/ant
tru'/cu/lent
tru'/ism
tru'ly
trum'/pet
trus/tee'

trust'/wor'/thy
try'/ing
tryst
tu·ber'/cu/lo'/sis
tu'bu/lar
Tuc/son', Ariz.
Tu'dor
Tues'day
tu·i'/tion
tulle
Tul'sa, Okla.
tum'/ble
tu'mult
tung'/sten
tu'nic
tun'/ing
tun'/nel/ing
tur'/ban
tur'/bid
tur'/bine
tur'/bo/jet'
tur'/bu/lence
tur'/gid
tur'/key
tur'/moil
tur'/nip
turn'/o'ver
turn'/pike'
tur'/pen/tine
tur'/pi/tude
tur'/quoise
tur'/tle

ıs'/sle
ı'tor
ıx · e'do
weez'/ers
welfth
welve
wen'ty—/five'
wi'/light'
witch
y'ing
ype'/writ'er
ype'/writ'/ing
type'/writ'/ten
ty'phoid
ty · phoon'
typ'/i · cal
typ'i · fy
typ'/ist
ty'po/graph'/i · cal
ty · pog'/ra/phy
ty · ran'/ni/cal
tyr'/an/nize
tyr'/an · ny (/nies)
ty'rant

U

ı · biq'/ui/tous
U · krai'/ni · an
u'ku/le'le
ul'cer
ul · te'/ri · or
ul'ti/mate
ul'ti/ma'/tum (/tums; /ma · ta)
ul'ti · mo
ul'tra/ma/rine'
ul'tra/mod'/ern
ul'tra/vi'o/let
um · bil'/i · cal
um'brage
um · brel'la
um'pire
un'ac/com'/mo/dated
un'ac/count'/a · ble
un'ad/vised'
un'af/fect'ed
un—A · mer'i · can
u'na/nim'/i · ty
u · nan'i/mous
un'a · void'/a · ble
un'a · ware'
un · bal'/anced
un'be/known'
un'be/liev'/ing
un · bi'/ased
un · can'ny

un · cer′/tain · ty
un · change′/a · ble
un · char′i/ta/ble
un′cle
un · col/lect′/i · ble
un · com′/fort/a · ble
un′ · con/di′/tion · al
un · con′/scion/a · ble
un · con′/scious
un · couth′
unc′/tu/ous
un′de/cid′ed
un′der/stand′/ing
un′der/tak′/ing
un′der way′
un′der/wear′
un′der/writ′er
un′di/vid′ed
un · doubt′/ed · ly
un′du/la′/tion
un · du′ly
un′ · em/ployed′
un′ · em/ploy′/ment
un′ · e/quiv′ · o/cal
un′ · fore/seen′
un · for′/tun/ate
un · gra′/cious
un · grate′/ful
un · health′y
u′ni/corn
u′ni/fi/ca′/tion
u′ni/form
u′ni/for′/mi · ty
u′ni · fy
u′ni/lat′/er · al
un′im/proved′
un′in/tel′/li/gent
un · in′/ter/est · ed
un′ion/ize
u · nique′
u′ni/son
u · nite′
u′ni · ty (/ties)
u′ni/ver′/sal
u′ni/verse
u′ni/ver′/si · ty (/ties)
un · kempt′
un · known′
un · learn′ed
un · men′/tion/a · ble
un · mer′/ci/ful
un · nat′u/ral
un · nec′/es/sar′ · y
un · oc′/cu/pied
un · or′/ga/nized
un · paid′
un · par′/al/leled
un · pleas′/ant
un · prec′e/dent′ed
un · prin′/ci/pled
un · print′/a · ble
un′pro/fes′/sion · al
un · prof′/it/a · ble
un · qual′i/fied

n·ques'/tion/a·ble
n·rav'el
n're/al'/i·ty (·ties)
n·rea'/son/a·ble
n're/spon'/sive
n·right'/eous
n·san'i/tar'y
n'sat/is/fac'/to·ry
n·sa'/vo·ry
n'sci/en/tif'ic
n·scru'/pu/lous
n·skilled'
n·sound'
n·think'/ing·ly
n·til'
n·time'ly
n·to'/ward
n·tu'/tored
n·u'su·al
n·u'su/al·ly
n·ut'/ter/a·ble
n·var'/nished
n·want'ed
n·war'y
n·whole'/some
n·wield'y
n·wor'/thy
n·writ'/ten
p·braid'
p·heav'al
p·hold'
p·hol'/ster

up'per/most
up·ris'/ing
up·roar'i/ous
up·root'
up'stairs'
up'—to—/date' *adj.*
up'ward
u·ra'/ni·um
ur'ban (pert. to city)
ur·bane' (suave)
ur·ban'/i·ty (·ties)
ur'chin
ur'gen·cy
ur'gent
urg'/ing
u'ri/nal'y/sis (/ses)
u'ri/nar'y
us'a·ble
use'/ful
ush'er
us'ing
u'su/al·ly
u'su/rer
u·surp'
u'sur/pa'/tion
u'su·ry (/ries)
u·ten'/sil
u'ter·us
u·til'i/tar'i·an
u·til'/i·ty (·ties)
u'ti/lize
ut'most

u·to'pia
ut'ter/ance
ut'ter·ly
ut'ter/most

V

va'can·cy (/cies)
va'cant
va'cate
va·ca'/tion
vac'/ci/nate
vac'/cine
vac'/il/late
va·cu'/i·ty (·ties)
vac'u/ous
vac'u·um
vag'a/bond
va'ga·ry (/ies)
va'gran·cy
va'grant
vague
vain (conceited)
va'lance, *n.* (drapery)
vale
val'e/dic/to'/ri·an
va'lence, *n.* (chemical)
val'/en/tine
val'et
val'/iant
val'id
va·lid'/i·ty
va·lise'
val'/ley
val'or
val'u/a·ble
val'u/a'tion
val'ue
val'u/ing
valve
val'/vu/lar
vam'/pire
Van/cou'/ver
van'/dal/ism
vane (weathercock)
van'/guard
va·nil'la
van'/ish
van'/i·ty (·ties)
van'/quish
van'/tage
vap'id
va'por
va'por·i/za'/tion
var'i/a·ble
vari·a'/tion
var'i/cose

var'i/e·gat'ed
va·ri'e·ty (/ties)
var'i/ous
var'/nish
var'y/ing
vas'/cu/lar
Vas'e/line
vas'/sal
Vat'i/can
vaude'/ville
vault
vaunt
veg'e/ta/ble
veg'e/ta'/tion
ve'he/mence
ve'hi/cle
ve·hic'u/lar
vein (blood vessel)
vel'/lum
ve·loc'/i·ty (·ties)
ve·lours'
vel'/ve/teen'
ve'nal
vend·ee'
ven'/dor
ve·neer'
ven'/er/a·ble
Ve·ne'tian
Ven'e/zue'la
ven'/geance
ven'i/son
ven'/om/ous
ve'nous
ven'/ti/late
ven'/tri/cle
ven/tril'o/quism
ven'/ture/some
ven'ue
ve·ra'/cious
ve·rac'/i·ty (·ties)
ve·ran'da
ver'/bal
ver/ba'/tim
ver/be'na
ver'/bi/age
ver/bose'
ver'/dant
ver'/dict
verge
ver'i/fi/ca'/tion
ver'i/fied
ver'i·fy
ver'i/si/mil'i/tude
ver'i/ta/ble
ver'/mi/cel'li
ver'/mi/fuge
ver/mil'/ion
ver'/min
Ver/mont'
ver/mouth'
ver/nac'u/lar
ver'/nal
Ver/sailles'
ver'/sa/tile

versed
ver'/sion
ver'/sus
ver'/te/bra (/brae)
ver'/tex (the top)
ver'/ti/cal
ver'/ti·go
ver'y
ves'i/cle
ves'/pers
ves'/sel
ves'/ti/bule
ves'/tige
ves/ti'/gial
vest'/ment
ves'/try (/tries)
vet'/er·an
vet'/er·i/nar'y (/ies)
ve'to (·toes)
vex·a'/tion
vi'a·ble
vi'a/duct
vi'and
vi·bra'/tion
vi'bra/tor
vi·car'i/ous
vice'—/con'sul
vice'—/pres'i·dent
vice'/roy
vi'ce ver'sa
vi·cin'/i·ty (·ties)
vi'cious
vi·cis'/si/tude
vic'/tim
vic/to'/ri/ous
vic'/to·ry (/ries)
vict'/uals
vid'e·o
vig'i/lance
vi·gnette'
vig'/or/ous
vil'/i·fy
vil'/lage
vil'/lain
vil'/lain·y (/ies)
Vin/cennes', Ind.
vin'/di/cate
vin/dic'a/tive
(exonerating)
vin/dic'/tive
(revengeful)
vin'e/gar
vin'/tage
vi'o/late
vi'o/lence
vi'o/let
vi'o/lin'
vi'per
Vir'gin Is'lands
Vir·gin'ia
vir'/ile
vir'/tu·al
vir'/tue
vir/tu·o'so (/sos)

vir'u/lence
vi'rus
vis'/age
vis'—/à—/vis'
vis/cos'/i·ty (·ties)
vis'/cus (vis'/cer·a)
vis'/i·ble
vis'i/bil'/i·ty (·ties)
vi'sion/ar'y (/ies)
vis'/it·a'/tion
vis'i/tor
vi'sor
vis'u/a·lize
vi·tal'/i·ty
vi'tal·ly
vi'ta/min
vi'ti/ate
vit'/ri·ol
vi·tu'/per·a'/tion
vi·va'/cious
viv'id
vix'en
vo·cab'u/la'ry (/ries)
vo'cal
vo·ca'/tion·al
vo·cif'/er/ous
vod'ka
vogue
voice'/less
void'/a·ble
voile
vol'a/tile
vol/ca'no (/noes)
vo·li'/tion
vol'/ley
volt'/age
Vol/taire'
volt'/me'/ter
vol'u/ble
vol'/ume
vo·lu'/mi/nous
vol'/un/tar'y
vol'/un/teer'
vo·lup'/tu/ous
voo'/doo/ism
vor'/tex (whirlpool)
vo'ta·ry (/ries)
vouch'er
vow'el
voy'/age
vul'/can/ize
vul'/gar
vul/gar'i·ty
vul'/ner/a·ble
vul'/ture
vy'ing

W ___ ___ ___ ___ ___ ___ ___

wa'fer
waf'/fle
wa'ger
wag'/gish
Wag/ne'/ri·an
wag'on
wain'/scot
wain'/scot/ing
waist (part of body)
wait'/ing
wait'/ress
waive (give up)
waiv'er (abandonment)
walk'ie—/talk'ie
wal'/let
wall'/eyed'
wal'/lop
wal'/low
wal'/nut
Wal'pole
wal'/rus
waltz
wam'/pum
wand
wan'/der/ing
wan'/ton·ly
warb'/ler
war'/den
ward'/robe'
ware
(product, except clothing)
ware'/house'
war'/fare
war'i·ly
war'/mon'/ger
warp
war'/rant
war'/ran·ty (/ties)
war'/ri·or
war'y
wash'/a·ble
Wash'/ing/ton
was'n't
was'/sail
wast'/age
waste
(use needlessly)
waste'/ful
wast'/rel
watch'/ful
wa'ter/mark'
wa'ter/mel'on
wa'ter/proof'

watt'/age
wave
(progressive movement)
wa'ver (sway)
wav'i/ness
wax'en
way'/bill'
way'/far'er
way'/lay'
way'/ward
weak, *adj.*
weak'/ness
wealth'y
weap'on
wear
(pert. to clothes; deterioration)
wear'/a·ble
wea'/ri·ly
wea'/ri/some
wea'/sel
weath'er, *n., v.*
weave
wedge
Wednes'day
week, *n.*
week'/day
week'/end
week'ly
wee'/vil
weighed
weight
weird
wel'/come
wel'/fare
well'—/be'ing
well'/spring
wel'/ter/weight
weren't
west'/er·ly
west'/ern
West'/ern·er
West Vir/gin'ia
wharf (wharves)
wharf'/age
what/ev'er
what'/so/ev'er
whee'/dle
wheel'/bar'/row
wheeze
whence
when/ev'er
where'/a·bouts'
where·as'
where·by'
where'/fore
wher/ev'er
where·in'
where·of'
where'/with·al
wheth'er, *conj.*
which/ev'er
whim'/per
whim'/si/cal

whip'/pet
whirl'/pool'
whisk'er
whis'ky
whis'/per/ing
whis'/tled
white'/ness
whit'/en/ing
white'/wash'
whith'er
whit'/tled
who/ev'er
whole'/heart'ed
whole'/sale'
whole'/some
whol'ly (completely)
whoop'ee
whoop'/ing cough
who's (who is)
whose
who'/so/ev'er
Wich'i·ta, Kan.
wick'/ed/ness
wide'/spread'
wid'ow
width
wield
wife (wives)
wig'/gle
wig'/wam
wild'cat'
wil'/der/ness
wild'/fire'
wild'/ness
Wilkes—/Bar're, Pa.
will'/ful
wil'/low·y
Wil'/ming/ton, Del.
Win'/ches'/ter, Mass.
wind'/mill'
win'/dow/pane'
wind'/shield'
wind'/tun'/nel
wing'/spread'
win'/ner
Win/net' ka, Ill.
win'/ning
win'/some
win'/ter/green'
wire'/less
Wis/con'/sin
wis'/dom
wise'/crack'
wise'ly
wish'/bone'
wis/te'/ri·a
wist'/ful
witch'/craft'
with/draw'al
with/hold'
with·in'
with/stand'
wit'/ness
wit'/ti/cism'

wiz'/ard
wiz'/ened
woe'/be/gone'
wolf (wolves)
wom'an (wom'en)
wom'/an/hood
won'/der/ful
won'/drous
wood'/craft'
wood'en
wood'/land'
wood'/peck'er
wood'/work'/ing
wool'en
wool'/gath'/er/ing
wool'ly
Worces'/ter, Mass.
work'/a·ble
work'a/day'
worked
work'er
work'/man/ship
work'/shop'
world'ly
worm'y
wor'/ried
wor'·ry (/ries)
wor'/ry/ing
worse
wor'/ship
wor'/ship·er
worst
wor'/sted
wor'/thi·ly
worth'/less
worth'/while'
wor'/thy
wouldn't
wound
wran'/gle
wrapped
wrap'/per
wrath'/ful
wreak
wreath, *n.*
wreathe, *v.*
wreck'/age
wrench
wrest
wres'/tle
wres'/tling
wretch
wretch'ed
wrig'/gle
wright
wring
wring'er
wrin'/kle
wrist'/lock'
write
writ'er
writhe
writ'/ing
writ'/ten

wrong'/ful
wrong'ly
wrought
wrung
Wyc'/liffe
Wy·o'/ming

X

xer/og'/ra/phy
X ray, *n.*
X—ray, *v.*, *adj.*
xy'lo/phone

Y

yacht'/ing
yachts'/man (men)
Yan'/kee
yard'/age
yawn'/ing
year'/book
year'/ling
year'ly
yearn'/ing·ly
yeast
yel'/low
yeo'/man (/men)
yes'/ter/day
Yid'/dish
yield
yield'ed
yo'gurt
yoke (a device)
yo'kel
yolk (part of egg)
yon'/der
youn'/ger
youn'/gest
young'/ster
yours
your/selves'
youth'/ful
Yo—Yo

Z

zeal'ot
zeal'/ous
ze'bra
ze'nith
ze'o/lite
zeph'yr
zep'/pe/lin
ze'ro (·ros)
zest'/ful
zig'/zag
zin'/nia
Zi'on/ism
zipped
zip'/per
zir'/con
zith'er
zo'di · ac
zo · di'a/cal
zom'bi
zo · na'/tion
zon'/ing
zo · og'/ra/phy
zo · o/log'/i · cal
zo · ol'o · gy
zoomed
Zou/ave'
zwie'/back
zy'mase

ENGLISH ESSENTIALS

WORD DIVISION

General Rule

Divide a word between syllables: ter/mi/na′/tion; con′/scious; sub/trac′/tion.

Exceptions

1. Do not divide a word before a single-vowel syllable: sep′a/rate; e·lim′i/nate.

   There are three exceptions:

   (1) When there are two consecutive single-vowel syllables, divide between the vowels: con/tin′u/a′tion.

   (2) Divide before the single-vowel syllable when it is the first syllable of a root word: dis′/u·nite′.

   (3) When the single-vowel syllable is part of one of the suffixes *—able, —ible, —icle, —acle,* or *—ity,* divide before the vowels:* charge′/a·ble; log′/i·cal.

* When the ending *-ity* is made plural, some authorities recommend dividing after the *i:* i/ties.

2. Divide hyphenated words only after the hyphen: first—/men′tioned.
3. Never divide a word so that only one or two letters stand alone:** a·round′; quan′/ti·ty; ca′pa/ble.
4. Never divide a word after a silent consonant: sub′tle.
5. Never divide contractions, abbreviations, and figures: would'n't; Y.M.C.A.; $1,750.25.
6. Avoid dividing words at the ends of more than two consecutive lines.
7. Avoid dividing capitalized words. (Divisions are shown in *Word Finder*, though not recommended.)
8. Avoid dividing the last word of a paragraph or the last word on a page.

SPELLING

If a word ends with

1. a consonant + *y*, change the *y* to *i* and add *es:* cities.
2. a vowel + *y*, just add *s:* attorneys.
3. silent *e*, keep the *e* and add the suffix beginning with a consonant: management. Exceptions: abridgment; acknowledgment; judgment.
4. silent *e*, usually drop the *e* before adding a suffix beginning with a vowel: striving; usable.

** Journalists and others setting print in narrow columns do divide words so that two letters stand alone.

5. a consonant preceded by a vowel, and is a one-syllable word, double the consonant before adding a suffix beginning with a vowel: running; shipping.
6. a consonant preceded by a vowel, double the consonant if the word has two syllables and is accented on the second syllable: controlling; transferred. *But* if the word is accented on the first syllable, do not double the consonant—traveling; canceled.
7. a double consonant, usually retain both consonants when adding a suffix beginning with a vowel: dismissing.
8. soft *ce* or *ge,* keep the full word when adding the suffixes *able* and *ous:* changeable; serviceable; courageous.
9. hard *c,* add *k* before adding a suffix beginning with a vowel: trafficked; shellacking.
10. *sion* or *tion,* change the ending to *ible* when making an adjective: division/divisible; collection/collectible. *But* if the word ends with *ation,* the adjective ending is *able:* laudation /laudable. (There are some exceptions.)

Other spelling helps:

1. After *c,* always use *ei:* deceive; receive. If the sound is *ay,* use *ei:* weigh; sleigh. In most other words, the order is *ie:* believe; relieve.
2. When words ending in double *l* are used as prefixes or suffixes, drop an *l:* all/almost; full /skillful.
3. On a derivative, if the accent shifts to the

first syllable, do not double the consonant: preferred/preference.

4. The hyphen is used to avoid confusion: bell-like; re-cover (to cover again).
5. These prefixes and suffixes join solidly: proof; like; semi; non; over; under—dustproof; businesslike; nonstop.
6. Note: supersede; exceed; proceed; succeed. All other words end with *cede*.

POSSESSIVES

1. The possessive of singular nouns is formed by adding an apostrophe and *s*.

   the girl's dress

2. A one-syllable word ending in *s* forms the possessive by adding an apostrophe and *s*.

   Mr. Jones's house

   NOTE: A word of more than one syllable ending in *s* or an *s* sound forms the possessive by adding an apostrophe only.

   Mr. Willis' desk

3. Plural nouns ending in *s* form the possessive by adding an apostrophe only.

   the Joneses' home   girls' hats

   NOTE: Plural nouns not ending in *s* form the possessive by adding an apostrophe and *s*.

   children's   men's

4. The possessive of compound words is added to the last word.

   father-in-law's

5. In the case of joint ownership, the possessive should be added to the last name.

   Baker and Black's new text

   NOTE: In the case of separate ownership, the possessive is added to each name.

   Billy's and Henry's bicycles

6. The possessive of appositives is formed by adding the possessive to the last word.

   Brown, the druggist's, business is prospering

7. A noun modifying a verbal noun must be in the possessive form.

   Do you approve of Jones's buying the business?

8. Avoid using the possessive form for inanimate objects.

   the door of the house

WORDS FREQUENTLY MISUSED

affect verb, to influence or act upon

effect verb, to bring about; noun, result

How will the policy affect our company?

What effect will this policy have on the company?

When do you expect to effect the change in policy?

anxious to be concerned
eager to look forward to

He is anxious about their safety.
They are eager to go to the picnic.

balance
rest
remainder
Use balance when referring to the balance of an account; otherwise use rest or remainder.

What is the balance of your account?
The rest (remainder) of the day we spent in the garden.

capital Chief; outstanding; financial resources; city
capitol Building in which a legislative body meets

compliment Congratulate; approval
complement That which fills up or completes
disinterested Without self-interest; unselfish
uninterested Not interested

We need disinterested people for the jury.
He is uninterested in his studies.

due to Use only to modify a noun or after a linking verb
because of On account of; owing to

Mr. Brown left because of a previous appointment.
The mistake was due to the clerk's incompetence.

expect to look for with confidence
suppose to imagine

suspect	to surmise; to be suspicious I expect him soon. I suppose it will be a difficult task. They suspected that he was the thief.
fewer **less**	Modifies plural nouns only Applies to quantity or bulk He has fewer children in class today than yesterday. We received less mail than usual.
leave **let**	to depart to allow He will leave soon. Let him go in your place.
liable **likely**	responsible, bound by law probably He will be liable for the cost of the suit. He is likely to arrive this afternoon.
like **as**	verb, preference for; preposition, identical with conjunction, since, to the same degree Your work is much like mine. He works much as I do.
percent **percentage**	Used immediately following the actual amount Denotes a portion of the whole The interest rate is 6 percent. What percentage of the allotment will you receive?
personal	Private, pertaining to a particular person

personnel	The body of persons employed in some service
	This book is based solely on his personal opinions.
	He is in charge of the office personnel.
principle	Rule; fundamental law
principal	Chief or main; leader or head; capital sum
	This is a simple bookkeeping principle.
	The principal of the school has resigned.
	The interest on the principal is due today.
	The principal cause of the strike is unknown.
some time	A period of time
sometime	An indefinite point of time
	It will take some time to repair the car.
	Please do come to see me sometime.
stationary	Fixed in a certain position
stationery	Writing paper
unless	Conjunction, except that
except	Preposition, with the exclusion of
	We will go unless I find some other plan.
	Everyone is going except Mary.
whether	Use when sentence involves a choice or doubt
if	A condition
	I do not know whether I shall go.
	He will go if he can.

NUMBERS

General Rule

Numbers of less than three digits should be written in full. Numbers of three digits or more should be written in figures.

Exceptions

1. Amounts of money should be written in figures (except in legal documents).

   $25 50 cents

2. Quantities and measurements are usually written in figures:

   2 percent
   policy No. 1276503
   98 degrees
   6:45 p.m.
   172 pounds
   49 bales
   90 feet
   9 by 12
   18 years old
   72 votes

3. Page numbers are written in figures.

   page 14

4. Simple fractions are usually written in words.

   One-half dozen will be sufficient.
   There are 12½ days in this quarter.

5. All street numbers except *One* are written in figures.

   26 East Oak Street
   One Madison Avenue

6. Spell out street names that are numbers up to *twelve.*

   The building is located at 140—142nd Street.
   We live at 12—25 Street.
   Drive slowly down Fifth Avenue.

7. When the date appears immediately after the month, express the date in figures. If the day of the month precedes the month, it may be written in figures or spelled out.

   Thank you for your letter of May 15.
   Your order of the 15th has not yet arrived.
   We do not have your letter of the sixth.

8. When several numbers are used in a sentence in similar construction, write all numbers in figures unless the numbers are all less than three digits.

   Similar construction: There were 149 children, 98 women, and 80 men.
   Different construction: The five machines were sold for $725.

9. When one number immediately follows another, spell out the smaller number and express the larger number in figures.

   I needed 32 three-cent stamps.
   She bought three 12-cent stamps.

10. When expressing time, it is better to spell out simple expressions and use numbers for less simple expressions.

    four o'clock   2:35

11. Numbers at the beginning of a sentence must be written in full.

12. Approximations should be written in full.
    He sells over ten thousand articles in his store.

CAPITALIZATION

1. Capitalize the names of individuals.
2. Capitalize a title of honor or respect immediately preceding a personal name.

   General Bradley Professor Wilson
3. Capitalize titles used in place of the name of a specific person.

   The Governor of Texas the Secretary of State

   NOTE: Do not capitalize titles not referring to specific persons.

   How many countries have presidents?
   All the professors are busy.
4. Capitalize the names of the months, days of the week, and holidays.

   January Monday Thanksgiving

   NOTE: Do not capitalize the seasons.

   fall, summer, winter, spring
5. Capitalize geographic names.

   Canada Mississippi River Pacific Ocean

   NOTE: Capitalize eastern, northern, western, etc. only when they are part of a proper noun designating a world division.

   East Germany Southern California
6. Capitalize east, west, north, and south when they refer to geographic divisions of the country.

   The Northwest the Deep South

NOTE: Do not capitalize such words when they refer to direction.

We went north five miles and then turned east.

7. Capitalize the names of courses of study or abbreviations of specific courses.

   B. A. 532 Principles and Problems in Education (exact title)

   NOTE: Do not capitalize subjects unless they are derived from proper nouns.

   shorthand history English American literature

8. Capitalize the names of associations, clubs, committees, commissions, companies, boards, departments, offices, schools, churches, etc. when they are used with a proper name.

   First Presbyterian Church Oklahoma State University General Products Company

9. Capitalize the names of monuments, buildings, parks, streets, etc.

   the Alamo Calderwood Hall Elm Street Central Park

10. Capitalize the following governmental bodies: municipal, state, or national bodies; legislative bodies; government (when used to refer to the United States government or any foreign government), and the words Army and Navy or any of their branches if part of the name.

    Congress (of the U.S.) the Army U.S. Naval Reserve the Government

11. Capitalize the first word of a direct quotation when it is a complete sentence.

John said, "Please give us a chance to show what we can do."

NOTE: Do not capitalize the first word of a quotation that is only a part of the entire sentence.

This machine is the only one that uses a "lifetime belt."

12. Capitalize all principal words in titles of books, magazines, newspapers, plays, reports, etc.

The History of the Typewriter

NOTE: The word *the* is capitalized only when it is the first word of a title.

PUNCTUATION

The Comma

1. Use commas to separate words and phrases in a series.

The secretary needs a supply of erasers, pens, pencils, and ink.

2. Use commas to separate the two main clauses of a compound sentence joined by a coordinate conjunction. (and, but, or, for, nor, neither, either, or, etc.)

Most of the men will arrive today, but a few will not come until later.

NOTE: Do not separate the parts of a compound predicate with a comma.

He studied the manual carefully and then wrote his term paper.

3. Use commas to set off a nonrestrictive clause.

That building, which is a well-known landmark here, is to be renovated.

NOTE: Also set off nonrestrictive participial phrases with commas.

Mr. Smith, having read his report to us, left the room.

Mary, believing her work was finished, went home.

NOTE: Do not use commas to set off restrictive clauses.

The book that helped me most was written by John McAnally.

4. Use a comma to set off an introductory adverbial clause from the rest of the sentence.

When Mr. Jones arrives, he should report to the president immediately.

NOTE: Transposed phrases containing verb forms and transposed infinitive phrases are also set off from the rest of the sentence with commas.

On the last page of the manuscript sent you yesterday, you will see the corrections.

To determine the best solution, we must study the facts.

NOTE: The following words often introduce adverbial clauses: although, if, because, as, whenever, whether, since, before, after, unless, as soon as, provided, when, while, etc.

5. Use a comma to set off a nonrestrictive adverbial clause from the rest of the sentence.

   We shall be glad to fill your order of the 10th, although you have not yet paid your account.

6. Use commas to set off nouns of direct address.

   I believe, Mr. Joy, that you will be well satisfied with this machine.

7. Use commas to set off explanatory or interrupting expressions in a sentence.

(a) Words used in apposition	Mr. Jones, my assistant, will help you.
(b) Geographical locations	Mr. Wilson, of Richmond, Indiana, is president.
(c) Abbreviations	Mr. F. L. Fletcher, Jr., will be the speaker.
	Mary Jones, Ed. D., will represent us.
(d) Dates	The Institute will meet August 10, 1980, in Erie.
(e) Parenthetical words, phrases and clauses	I think, therefore, that we should continue.
	The men, as you know, are dissatisfied.

8. Use a comma to set off a quoted sentence from the rest of the sentence.

   "What we must know," the speaker continued, "is readily apparent."

9. Use commas to show the omission of words within the sentence.

   Mr. Black will arrive this morning; Mr. Armstrong, this afternoon.

The Semicolon

1. Use a semicolon to separate two coordinate clauses in a sentence when they are not joined by a conjunction.

   Taxes are higher than ever before; they should be reduced.

   NOTE: Very short clauses may be separated with commas.

   The men worked, the women cooked, and the children played.

2. When one or both of the coordinate clauses within a sentence contain commas, use a semicolon to separate the clauses.

   The people, I believe, are ready to accept the plan; we should act now.

   We should investigate the matter thoroughly; however, there must be no delay.

3. When a sentence contains a series of word groups punctuated by commas, the groups may be separated by semicolons to facilitate reading.

   Those present included John Norton, of Iowa City; Halton Hill, of Indianapolis; William Wilks, of Tampa; and Jack Jordan, of Milwaukee.

The Colon

Use the colon after the introduction to a long quotation, a list, or an enumeration.

At the meeting Mr. Jones reported: "Membership has increased 50 percent this past year."

The qualities I must have in a secretary are these: efficiency, courtesy, intelligence, and dependability.

The Hyphen

1. A hyphen is usually used between two or more words serving as a single adjective before a noun.

   first-class ticket   up-to-date text

   NOTE: When these words follow the noun, they are not hyphenated.

   The text is up to date.

   NOTE: When an adverb ending in *ly* is used with an adjective or participle, the compound is not hyphenated.

   A poorly conducted meeting

2. Use a hyphen in compound numbers written as words.

   forty-two

   NOTE: The hyphen is also used between the numerator and denominator of a fraction written in words unless one of the elements contains a hyphen or the fraction is used as a noun.

   one-half interest   twenty-three hundredths   one half of the book

Quotation Marks

1. Use quotation marks to enclose direct quotations.

   The speaker said, "You should remember we have no time to lose."

   NOTE: Periods and commas should be placed inside the quotation marks; semicolons and colons, outside.

2. Words or phrases in a sentence may be enclosed in quotation marks when the writer desires to call attention to them.

   Most of us spend entirely too much time on "trivia."

3. When a quotation consists of more than one paragraph, put quotation marks at the beginning of each paragraph but only at the end of the last paragraph.

4. Enclose a quotation within a quotation in single quotation marks.

   "I still remember," Mark said, "the motto on that wall: 'Laugh and the world laughs with you; weep and you weep alone.' "

5. Use quotation marks to enclose the titles of articles, chapters in a book, or titles of brief monographs and booklets.

The Dash

1. Use the dash to indicate an abrupt change in thought.

   Do you remember—but of course you don't.

2. Use a dash to set off an appositive expression that includes commas.

   Every week there are so many demands on his time—committee meetings, appointments, conferences, speeches—that he is becoming exhausted.

3. Use a dash to set off a disconnected expression which interrupts the sentence.

   The house we are building—there's none other like it—is nearly finished.

4. When expressions like *namely, for example that is,* and so on begin a complete idea, use the semicolon before and a comma after. If such expressions are followed by an incomplete idea, use the dash before and the comma after.

4 5 6 7 8

NSF GS 1297 Research
Acct. No. 3-5040-35-1457